Beautiful Jewel

JALANA SHEREE WALSH

Cover Photo courtesy of Heather Murray owner of 876 Studios
www.876studios.com

Copyright © 2015 JaLana Sheree Walsh

ISBN:1514188368
ISBN-13: 978-1514188361

DEDICATION

To every person that's been victimized:

Every time you remember, every time you struggle, every time you feel that
your heart is breaking under the weight of what happened to you,
ask Him (*Jesus Christ*) to help you. ~By David Powlison

CONTENTS

ACKNOWLEDGMENTS

To my husband, Chadwick. For over 20 years you have proven your love to me. Thank you for not only being my husband, thank you for remaining my best friend. I love you with all my heart.

To my children, Andrew, Rachel and Christina. After being told by doctors I would never be able to have children, God blessed me with three of the most amazing gifts from heaven. I love you all so much and I'm thankful every day that I get to be your mother.

1

November 11th

A tuft of brown curls swayed in front of small, brown eyes searching frantically for a place to hide. She glanced behind her and looked down the darkened hallway with a smile on her lips and a laugh caught in her throat. The queen of hide and seek, she had left the main room with the other kids and wasn't going to get caught first like the last time.

She wasn't sure where the hallway led, but she knew no one would think to search for her here. It was sort of off limits, but it didn't stop her. In a muffled voice past the door she had pushed through, she heard Kirk, another young boy, counting. He counted fast and skipped numbers. After a moment, the counting stopped, and ended abruptly with a loud shout of, "Ready or not, here I come!"

The little girl grew frantic. She ran to the door at the tail end of the hallway and grabbed the knob. It twisted freely. Opening the door, she passed through and stopped. Before her were stairs that led down. This staircase was darkened, but at the bottom landing she could see that the room below was lit. She heard something, muffled sounds and whimpers that sounded like a plea.

She opened her mouth to call out, but no sound came. Instead, in small steps, her feet moved forward, taking the stairs one at a time. With each movement towards the last stair, the world grew brighter and brighter. She heard a deep grunt, much deeper than any child could produce. It stopped her. She was scared.

Fear tightened in her chest, but her feet inched forward, curiosity tugging her forward. She wondered what the low whine was, the weak plea for relief. Someone else was down here. Were they lost or hurt? Her toes lingered on the bottom step, and she peeked around the wall on the left which concealed the rest of the room. Her eyes widened with fear and shock. The light brightened beyond what was normal, before dimming suddenly to darkness.

Jewel opened her eyes slowly. She stared into the darkness of her bedroom. Allowing her head to fall lazily to the right, she spied her alarm clock. Bright green fuzzy numbers slowly came into focus. 4:32 a.m.

Reluctantly, she pulled her sweating body up and swallowed back the lingering fear she felt from the little girl. Her breath was hollow and shaky, her throat dry and crisp. She was sure she wouldn't have been able to talk even if she wanted to.

Sliding from her bed, she forced her legs to move her body towards the bathroom. Once inside, she reached for the light switch with a limp arm and stiff fingers. Her eyes pulsed in pain as her pupils dilated. After they had adjusted, Jewel met her brown eyes in the mirror. Dark, wavy hair cascaded around her face.

Some might have said she had the tousled look that men loved. Personally, she thought she just looked worn down. She saw the puffiness in her eyes and the tinge of red attesting to her fatigue creeping at the corners of her retinas. With a tired sigh, Jewel shook her thoughts away and reached for the sink knob. She turned on the cold water.

Dipping her hands into the bitingly cold liquid, she felt her body begin to recover from what she saw. A shiver clawed its way over her body. Ignoring it, she splashed the pooled water from her hands over her face. Like being slapped with ice, Jewel trembled, allowing noise from her throat to escape. She could already tell the day was going to be rough. Still, she knew she'd get a handle on it. She always did.

Jewel moved through the worn path trodden down to a dull dirt passage with ease and familiarity. She moved with a purpose, barely noticing two elementary school-aged children weaving in and out of the tombstones with small American flags in their hand. Absently, she ran the tips of her fingers across several stones before she spotted her destination.

Visiting her mother always tugged deeply at Jewel's heart. Bright, sunny days made it even more difficult. Kneeling before the gray stone, Jewel lowered her head in reverence. She pulled a small bouquet of flowers from her shoulder bag. Taking a moment to breathe in the scent of the flowers, she closed her eyes. She struggled to keep tears at bay, breathing deeply before she opened her eyes again and laid the flowers down.

"Happy birthday, Mom," she whispered. Her voice floated thinly on the warm air. A jarring ring shattered the moment, yanking

Jewel from her thoughts. Grabbing her cell phone from her hanging bag, Jewel felt her gut churning before she even caught a glimpse of the time.

She was late. Again. Turning to leave in a whirl, Jewel ran into something tall and strong. Confused, she stumbled back. She met light blue eyes and a blonde and brown speckled hairline of an older man.

With ease, the man bent down, taking her bag by the handles into his hands. He smiled kindly, offering Jewel the bag. Stammering, she grabbed her purse and shouldered it roughly. She muttered a weak, "Thank you," as she met the man's eyes. "I'm sorry, Sir. I didn't see you there."

"It's quite okay," he said with smooth elegance as he stepped aside to allow room for Jewel to pass. The movement jogged her memory and she remembered she was late.

"Thank you, again," she called over her shoulder. She grabbed onto the straps of her purse to keep it steady as she walked and glanced over her shoulder for one last glimpse of the man before she broke into a trot towards her curbside-parked car.

Over her medium heels pounding into the dirt, Jewel heard the ring of her cell phone again. She remembered that she had never answered it the first time. At this hour, there were only two people that were likely to be vying for her attention: David or her boss, Mr. Pierce.

Jewel slipped her hand into her purse and quickened her pace; her heart skipped as she glanced at the image displaying on the wide surface screen of her smartphone. It was David. Her thumb hesitated over the green to accept the incoming call momentarily before she swiped and answered the call. She tucked the phone between her shoulder and ear, Jewel reached for her keys. Perhaps if she seemed busy enough, David would end the call sooner than later.

"Hey, babe," she said, doing her best to breathe heavily into the phone, "I'm heading to my car right now," she paused to press the unlock button on her car's remote. No sooner than she had pressed the smooth silicon button she heard the familiar call of her car answering back with two short beeps. She had hoped in the silence and purposeful shuffling that David would speak up. Instead, only silence greeted her from the line. "David, are you there?"

"If you decide to cancel, maybe you should let me know so I'm not waiting for you, wondering where you went or what went wrong."

Jewel grimaced and slipped her fingers into the hook of her car. "Decide to cancel? What are you talking—," Jewel gasped. They had a dinner date at seven at Silent Meadow restaurant. "That was for November tenth, baby. What day is it?" No sooner than the words escaped her lips, Jewel felt her heart begin to sag with a heavy weight. There was silence on the other end. How could she have forgotten? Jewel searched the wide front window for a hint of how to salvage the situation. There was nothing—and then she thought of a solution.

"Baby, let me make it up to you. Tonight. Same place, same time. I'll be there, I promise."

"You always promise," David's voice sounded softly through her phone's receiver. It caused Jewel's heart to ache even more.

"As soon as I hang up, I'll put a reminder—hold on," Jewel pulled the phone from her head and stared at the glassy screen. Mr. Pierce was calling. "Oh shoot, David. My boss is calling. I won't forget, baby. Meet me there, okay? I need to get this," Jewel removed the phone from her ear and swapped the calls. She shoved her keys into the ignition and readied to pull off.

Even if she hadn't visited her mother like this, her mornings were still the same, rushed and hurried with an upset call from David every three or four days. She knew she needed to get a better handle on her time, but it was next to impossible with how little she had been sleeping at night.

"Good morning, Mr. Pierce," Jewel forced her most professional voice. She heard his sigh and then she heard his voice.

"How many times do I need to talk to you about your time?"

Jewel rolled her eyes, happy she wasn't having the conversation face to face. "I know, I know. I'm on my way right now. Give me five minutes and I'll be there."

"There are some things I need to run by you once you get here," he began.

"Okay, your office first—got it." Jewel hurried their conversation. "Let me focus on the road and I'll be there as soon as possible."

It wasn't all that soon, however; with her Prius getting lost in the ambient hustle of the late morning traffic rush hour, it was nearly fifteen minutes before she saw her work building break into view over the horizon, a two-story building of light brown stone on the edge of downtown in the bustling city.

Her car had barely stopped before she had the door open with an outstretched foot ready to grab concrete. She wiggled the keys from the ignition and grabbed her handbag as she slammed the door closed, leaping from the car in a huff of breath. Before she rounded the building's corner towards the double front doors, she dropped her right arm back and pointed the remote lock towards the car. She pressed the right button without even glancing behind her and heard the call of her car.

Breaking out into a trot, she rushed past the secretary, barely noticing the dark-skinned young woman engaged in conversation with a male co-worker. Jewel's passing breeze ruffled a small stack of papers on the top of the secretary's desk. A few sheets floated to the ground, but Jewel continued towards Mr. Pierce's office.

No sooner than she had entered, she held her hands up in protest. "There was a huge accident on I-95. I wouldn't have even been on the interstate for longer than five minutes but after the lanes had backed up—," she fell silent as Mr. Pierce slowly lifted a hand with a kind smile.

"I know you, Jewel. Five minutes is closer to fifteen than anything else," with a deep frown, he stared at her at length. "Your tardiness is an issue though." Jewel bit her lip. "Thank you for stopping in," he continued. After a pause of thought, he added, "How are you today?"

Jewel shrugged her shoulders, slightly baffled by the question. "I'm all right," she said blankly. "Why wouldn't I be?"

Mr. Pierce was a middle-aged man with dark sun spots on his forehead and cheeks. He pressed his lips together in a soft frown and raised a brow. "Are you sure, Jewel? Today is—."

Jewel interrupted with a quick shake of her head and a wave of her hand. "I'm fine," she sniffed, her eyes widening. Mr. Pierce's gaze failed to change. "I'm all right, Mr. Pierce. Really," she emphasized, letting her face relax. "I just got off to a late start this morning," with a smile, Jewel whipped her dark mid-length hair over her shoulders. Short curls framed the front of her face. "I'm here now and I'm ready to work," Jewel concluded with a firm nod.

After another moment more of hesitation, Mr. Pierce took a deep breath through his small mouth. "Okay. Before I let you go, how's your newest client?"

Jewel felt a heaviness begin to settle over her. She thought of the young teen whose case she had just opened the previous week. "Nothing much has changed," she said solemnly. In an instant, her face hardened and she began to nod with determination. Meeting Mr. Pierce's gaze, she continued, "I've been racking my brain for ways I might be able to get some headway." She searched his face as she spoke, "I'm hoping for a breakthrough soon."

Satisfied, Mr. Pierce nodded with a smile brushing his lips. "That's good. I'm glad to hear that." He pointed at her absently before leaning back in his plush computer chair. For a moment, his eyes drifted towards his obscured computer screen. "Her case is real complex so stay on it, Jewel." He smiled widely, glancing towards Jewel momentarily, "I'm sure we'll see changes soon."

"I sure hope so," Jewel muttered, shifting the weight on her feet. She really needed to get going.

As if sensing Jewel's growing anticipation, Mr. Pierce sat up quickly and grabbed a folder from his desk. "Alright, before you head out," he held the folder out to Jewel. She took it and slipped it into her bag without hesitation. "Please remember to get me those case studies by Friday."

"Of course," Jewel held up a hand as she stepped backward towards the door. "Okay, see you later," she turned from the office and headed down the hall, taking a deep breath. Her day had officially begun.

2

Another Day at Work

Hours later at a break in between sessions, Jewel sat in her office, a stuffy room with one window. She let out a sigh and moved her hair from her shoulders onto her back. Her body ached. Placing a hand on her neck, she rubbed her neck with firm fingers. She still had two hours left in the day and a support group meeting in one hour. It wasn't likely she'd be able to clear her mind long enough to work on the case studies.

She ran the palms of her hands over her face and pushed herself from the computer chair, heading out her office. In the hallway, she stopped at the water fountain and pushed on the gray bar to release the water. It was cold. Using the machine made it hum seconds later. Although the refreshing temperature helped settle her nerves, the water carried with it a tart aftertaste.

Jewel stood and gasped. There was a man standing in front of her with a loose flowing shirt hanging off his body. Narrowing her eyes, Jewel straightened herself and swallowed the remaining water in her mouth. "What is it now, Ronald?"

"You alright, Jewel?" His voice was a tone between deep and mid-range, almost attractive, but not quite deep enough. "I saw you rush into work earlier. You looked really upset."

Jewel produced a tight smile with pressed lips. "Just a little late, Ronald," she looked away and turned her eyes down the corridor. "If you'll excuse me—."

He interrupted her, the concern his voice previously held suddenly gone. "What about our date, baby? When you gon let me take you out?" He laughed and stepped in front of her as she tried to move away.

Pausing, Jewel grimaced and crossed her arms. Ronald was just a year older and just as educated. He had a heart for the children they helped at the counseling center, but he had a weakness. "Ronald," Jewel met his eyes without further hesitation, "I will never go out on a date with you."

Putting his hands on his chest, Ronald was shocked. "Now that's just mean, Jewel. Why you gotta be like that?"

Rolling her eyes, Jewel's scowl deepened. "And you're way too educated to talk like that. I'm in a relationship, Ronald. You know that."

He shrugged his shoulders. "What does that have to do with me?"

Shaking her head, Jewel held Ronald's gaze firmly. "You see that?" She pointed at him, "That's the real reason I could never date you. You don't respect me."

"Girl, you know I respect you!" Ronald said with a laugh. His eyes danced, ignoring Jewel's growing annoyance. "I respect your pretty brown eyes. Those puffy red lips," as he began to look her body over, Jewel shook her head, and gently pushed past him.

"This conversation is over," she half chuckled to herself as Ronald continued, behind her now.

"I respect every ounce of you, baby," he paused, "Just one date, Jewel. One date!" He called after her. Jewel didn't bother with a reply. She headed towards the front desk near the double doors. Meeting the eyes of the young secretary, Kiara, Jewel let out a held breath.

"Is Landra in her office?" The woman smiled and gestured down an adjacent hall. Rapping on the desk with the tips of her knuckles, Jewel smiled. "Thanks a bunch," she turned towards the hallway. After a brief glance around, she saw that Ronald had retreated to his office. Shaking her head with a grin, Jewel headed towards the lone office at the beginning of the hallway. After a soft knock, she let herself in. She heard Landra on the phone.

Landra was a lanky blond with alluring emerald eyes and a bright smile. She motioned to Jewel to sit down with a weak flick of her hand, "Those are definitely some things I can take into consideration," Landra said into the receiver. She continued her conversation without skipping a beat. Turning towards the computer screen, she pecked at the keyboard. "Okay, yes. I have it. Thank you. I'll call you after our next meeting once I've had time to," Landra paused and eyed Jewel playfully. She rolled her eyes with an exaggerated head roll and used her free hand to mimic talking.

"Okay, yes, yes. That's fine. Great," Landra opened her mouth and let it hang open in feigned exasperation as if waiting for a chance to pounce with her closing line. "Alright, that sounds wonderful. My next appointment is here so I need to oh—okay," Landra met Jewel's eyes again, rousing a chuckle as she widened her eyes. "And thank you again. I'll be calling you in a couple days. Okay, bye-bye," Landra removed the phone quickly and let a laugh rip through the air.

"Girl, you are so crazy," Jewel chuckled, relaxing into the chair opposite her friend's desk. She felt a heaviness begin to lift while in her friend's presence.

"Ms. Abby can talk for days," Landra grinned. "So what's up?" She crossed her arms and put her elbows on the desk.

Jewel allowed herself a laugh. She felt her muscles unwind. "Ran into Ronald," she paused, "again."

Landra's eyes sparkled. "Tell me something I don't already know," she leaned back in her chair and glanced around the room. "That man's been after the two of us for years."

"Hmm," Jewel crossed her legs and loosely examined her fingernails, "he has a little charm," her voice was flat, "I'll give him that."

"A little charm is right," Landra agreed and took a deep breath, "but he'll need more than that to make us look twice," she giggled with Jewel. After a moment, Landra's smile faded. "Did you go to the grave site this morning?"

Jewel let her eyes drop back to her nails, finding a sudden fascination with them. She loved her relationship with Landra, but some days she knew she wasn't strong enough to be transparent. Jewel bit back a fit of emotion. Her eyes began to burn and she repeatedly blinked, forcing herself to meet Landra's eyes. She started with a slow nod.

"That's why I was late today," she sniffed and looked away with a flick of her eyes before snapping her eyes back to Landra's. "You'd think I'd be over this by now."

Landra's eyes softened. "You take all the time in the world," she whispered.

Shaking her head slightly, Jewel looked away. She stared towards the ground and saw nothing in particular. "I still hurt when I think of her. It's as if it hasn't been years but like I just found out last week," Jewel chuckled nervously at herself. "I feel so pathetic."

Landra stood up and quickly moved to Jewel's chair. She squatted down and placed a hand on Jewel's arm. She waited until Jewel faced her. "She died young," her voice had changed, "and at a time when you still needed her."

Jewel let the words sink in. After a breath, she nodded. Her mother hadn't been very old at all when she breathed her last. This was the reality she needed to remind herself of when she started mourning her loss. It was okay to still be upset. It was okay to still wish her mother was around. It was okay to still miss her.

"You know," Jewel looked towards Landra, "I used to think 47 was so old when I was younger," she smirked. "Now I'm in my thirties and," she paused.

"Now you realize just how young she really was," Landra finished, rubbing Jewel's arm softly. Jewel nodded, unable to say more. After a moment, Landra tapped Jewel's arm and stood. "I have something for you. They came while you were at lunch."

Landra turned towards her desk. She walked to the front and stopped just before she came to the right edge hidden from

Jewel. Bending over the corner of the desk, she reached down and groped for something. When she stood again, she held a small bouquet of dark red roses.

Jewel's eyes widened, her mouth falling open. "Those are beautiful," she said, reaching out for them. She eagerly read the note attached to the square card. "David," she said out loud. She smiled and then brought the roses to her nose so that she could smell them. "Oh, he's so sweet," she breathed, closing her eyes as she smelled the roses again. This time, she thought of his strength and loving gaze. David was a strong man with coffee-colored skin with a patch of neatly trimmed stubble on his chin.

Landra smiled as she watched her friend. She retreated to her desk and sat down slowly with her palms on her desk. "So are we going to do lunch tomorrow or what?"

Jewel pulled her gaze from the flowers. "Oh, yes. I'm sorry I ate without you, girl," she smiled and looked towards the roses again. "I needed some air and completely forgot. I have dinner with David tonight," Jewel's smile fell as she met Landra's eyes. "I completely forgot our date last night."

Landra's mouth dropped. "You didn't," she shook her head.

With a weak nod and grimace, Jewel nodded. "I didn't even remember until he called me about it this morning."

"What is wrong with you?"

Jewel sighed and looked away. She didn't have an excuse for her spotty memory lately. She had always struggled with time management, but never like she had been lately. "Maybe I just need to start using a better planner?" She tried to laugh off the settling silence, but Landra's face didn't change.

"You've got a good man, Jewel."

"I know, I know," Jewel leaned forward over her crossed legs. "I know I do," she breathed softly. "I just need some time to clear my head," Jewel squeezed her eyes shut. Her mind drifted to the dream that had awoken her last night. "Once I start sleeping better…" Jewel met Landra's gaze and nodded firmly, "once I start sleeping better, things will be better. How's Hannah feeling?" Jewel asked, switching topics seamlessly.

Landra didn't move. She held Jewel's eyes solemnly for several seconds and then relaxed. After the silence between them had swelled, Landra sighed and leaned back. "Yeah, Hannah is much better. She was able to go back to school today."

Jewel smiled. "That's good," she nodded her head genuinely. "I'm glad," glancing towards her watch, Jewel used the moment to end their conversation. She knew Landra too well and if she stayed any longer, their talk wasn't likely to be any more comfortable than the last two minutes were. "Well, I need to get started prepping for my group this afternoon," Jewel stood and quickly put her back to Landra. She knew her friend was still disappointed.

Heading towards the door, Jewel continued, "Remind me that we'll do lunch tomorrow, and I'll catch up with you later, okay?" She slipped through the door, forcing her eyes forward as she left. She didn't need to look back to know that Landra was likely still frowning.

JALANA SHEREE WALSH

3

Dealing with Guilt

"Did you know that there are several types of guilt?" Jewel asked, standing just outside the closed circle of a group of teenaged girls. Their faces stared back at her, hanging on her words. A few shifted uncomfortably in their chairs. Slipping into the only empty chair in the ring, Jewel crossed her legs and took a moment to run her eyes over each of the girl's faces.

"It's just one of the many emotions that victims feel," Jewel continued. She reached towards the nearest girl and placed a warm hand on her knee. She met the young woman's eyes and gave her knee a gentle squeeze. "It's also one of the most difficult to identify."

Jewel turned from the girl to face the others in the circle. "Often times you'll actually believe the guilt. It sounds like many things. The most common are thoughts that help you think you had it coming because you were there, wearing that dress, or—."

"Decided to drink the beer," one woman spoke up.

"I just wanted to make out," another softly whispered.

Jewel nodded eagerly at all the comments. "Absolutely. You've probably struggled with feeling like somehow you asked for this, right?" In the circle of five girls, they each nodded their heads slowly. Jewel watched as their faces brightened with the knowledge. They looked at each other in the circle with a strange curiosity. "How many of you have dealt with or still struggle thinking this way?" Each of their hands lifted to the sky pensively. Jewel nodded and then turned towards the first girl she had initially touched.

"This is Michelle," Jewel turned to the brown haired teen housing a dusting of freckles on her face, "she's been here for a while and I've been able to help her extensively through this stage," she paused. "Would you mind sharing your story with the new girls here today, Michelle?"

Nodding, Michelle locked her thick hair behind her ears and turned into the circle. She took her time, looking at each face before she opened her mouth to speak.

"Well, for a long time I thought it was my fault," she spoke with a rich accent. "Sometimes, I still feel like maybe it was my fault," she drew out the words thoughtfully. "The difference is that now, I know when I have those thoughts that it's not true."

Michelle's legs were folded beneath her chair, her knees touching each other. Her hands rested in her lap. She began to wring them together, tugging on her fingers as she continued. "You see, I was always a big flirt. I never thought anything about it, really," she breathed heavily, glancing up periodically to still make brief eye contact.

"I thought it was just fun, and it made me feel good about

myself when a guy flirted back with me." Meeting the eyes of the other girls in the group, Michelle continued as she saw them nodding their heads in agreement. "For me, it was innocent and I didn't really think it could be anything other than that."

She stopped talking, squeezing her hands together tightly. Jewel rubbed her leg, hoping to give her strength to continue. After a moment, Michelle ran her fingers through her hair and took a deep breath.

"There was a guy I had a crush on for a long time," she chuckled, "Like over a year." The small faces nodded, hanging on her every word. "He never seemed to notice me before that night," she sniffed, swallowing back an obstacle in her throat.

After a moment, she shook her head, "Sometimes, I still wonder why. I wonder why I didn't just leave him alone, why I cared about him so much. Why?" She looked towards the other girls as if they possibly had the answer. When no one responded, she continued. "I was going to a party and I knew he was going to be there. I wanted to look cute, so I dressed up real nice," she nodded, affirming herself.

"I used to think that this is where it was my fault," Michelle nodded as her eyes glassed over with the memory. "I dressed up for him—I asked for it." Taking a deep breath, she ran her fingers through her hair. The other girls in the room leaned forward in their chairs, waiting for Michelle to continue.

"I know those thoughts are wrong, but I still have them." After another moment of strained silence, Michelle pushed herself forward. "He also had a girlfriend I knew would be there, so my interest didn't really seem to make sense. Except, this night, everyone could hear their fight," as the memory pulled Michelle into the past, her words fell into a steady rhythm of speech.

"They broke up and after she left, he seemed so sad, I," she shook her head, and shrugged her shoulders, "I walked over to him. I think I was probably a little past tipsy at this point—but I know I wasn't drunk. I wanted to be sure he was okay. I tried to make small talk." Michelle's voice broke as she wrestled with continuing.

"I can't tell you how many times I've thought back to that night and wished I never crossed the room to be at his side," she sniffed and shook her head again, a sob escaping the confines of her throat, "but I did. I flirted with him and he flirted back. I touched his shoulder, he touched me back. We talked for what seemed like hours, I didn't even know people were leaving," she covered her mouth, holding in a larger cry.

Jewel squeezed the young woman's shoulder, her heart filling with sadness. She turned to look over the other girls in the group. They each seemed to be reliving the painful moment of their own torture. Taking a deep breath, she nodded. "Thank you for sharing," she began to whisper, but Michelle held up a firm hand.

"I want to finish," she said quickly, wiping at her face. "It hurts but I want the girls," Michelle stopped and faced the other eyes staring back at her from the inner circle. "I want you to know that there will come a day when things aren't as hard as they are now," she steadied her breathing with difficulty before continuing her story.

"I didn't realize people were leaving until I saw an old friend of his. Right before his friend stepped out the door I saw a strange look on his face. I didn't understand it, but he turned to me and," she paused, eyes widening, "and that's when it happened."

Bodies began to shift in their seats. Still, the women leaned in and listened intently. Michelle's face glistened under the fluorescent lights of the room. More tears streamed down her face, but she didn't stop this time.

"He held me down and raped me," her voice broke as a second sob escaped. "I begged him to stop. I called for help," her shoulders heaved up and down. She shook her head, her eyes sad. "No one heard me. I wasn't strong enough to fight him off of me and after I awhile, I just froze under him." Michelle fought hard to keep her composure. When she looked around the room, she saw others crying with her.

"Afterward, when I thought about that whole night, I couldn't stop thinking about the fact that I went to him. I pursued him. He didn't pursue me." Wiping at her face, strength returned to Michelle's voice.

With a sniff, she continued to speak, "I had been drinking and was flirting with him—I told him I wanted to have sex. That's what I used to think, but I know it's not true. I never said I wanted to sleep with him and I told him again and again," she stressed her words by pushing a fist into an open palm. The sound resonated in the room over sniffles, "I told him over and over to please stop. I begged him to stop, but he didn't listen."

Jewel handed Michelle a tissue from a box resting in between their two chairs. Michelle was a strong woman. She may not have thought or believed it at the time, but Jewel knew it took incredible strength to share like she had.

"Thank you, Michelle," turning from the young woman, Jewel faced the rest of the glistening faces from the group. "Michelle's been with us for several months now," she started with a nod. "We've worked hard with her and helped her to work through so much of what happened," after a pause, Jewel asked, "How many of you can relate to her thoughts?" Every girl raised a weak, limp hand. Jewel smiled kindly at each of them in turn. "Every person who has ever been violated sexually struggles with guilt."

Standing, Jewel moved behind the chair. She held the eyes of each teen in the room. "They feel that they must have done something to deserve the treatment they received. This is even true of victims of physical abuse—but no one ever has the right to violate your body. Ever." She stressed the last word with confidence. "Your body is yours. It belongs to you, and no one has the right to touch it without your consent." Jewel wiped her hands on her pants and moved to the back of the chair she had sat in earlier. "Okay, let's take out our journals," she began to walk around the grouped circle of chairs, eying the window along the back of the room.

Looking back to the girls, Jewel took a deep breath and let her voice carry through the room. "I want you to think about your different experiences, and write down some of the thoughts of guilt you've had. We're going to break them down and discuss them." She watched as arms dipped beneath their seats slowly, each one bringing up a different colored notebook and pen. Papers began to rustle as journals opened.

Jewel continued to speak, "Try to be as open and honest as you can about your feelings and thoughts. We're going to take turns examining them so that you'll know how to combat these very same feelings when you're alone and by yourself."

As the girls began to write in their journals, the room fell into silence by several degrees. All that could be heard was the scratching against paper. Jewel gave the girls a last glance before she moved to the window and peered outside. There was a car idling curbside. She ignored it and looked at the surrounding passing traffic in front of the office.

Talking about guilt always took a toll on her. She had her own amount of guilt that held her heart hostage and made it difficult to breathe some days. She caught her breath and noticed that her heart rattled within her heaving chest. Swallowing back a sandpaper lump in her throat, Jewel turned. The girls seemed to have stopped writing long ago. Their journals lay open across their lap and they each stared at Jewel with inquisitive eyes. Forcing a smile, Jewel found her most upbeat voice.

"Are you all done?" The girls nodded in unison, moving in their chairs as some flicked their hair and others stretched and arched their backs. "Okay. Debbi, how about we start with you? Is that okay?"

Debbi was a bright skinned woman with hazel eyes. She was eager to receive healing but lacked a ton of confidence. She smiled and lifted a hand with a pencil woven between her fingers. After locking a piece of hair behind her ears, the young woman began to speak. Her voice was lost to Jewel as her mind drifted back what had just happened to her. She was sure she was on the brink of a panic attack.

4
"Grandpa-No!"

Jewel steered the car into the parking garage of the complex. Even with her eyes open, they burned and ached to be rested. The lack of sleep from the night before began to weigh on her. As she left her car, she locked it remotely and started to head towards the elevator.

At the elevator's chrome doors, she rummaged through her handbag. Her fingers found the rectangular body of her phone and she grabbed it, pulling it out. After flicking through multiple screens, she sighed. No texts or messages.

The elevator bell sounded and seconds later, the doors opened from the center. A tall, thin white man accompanied by a shorter Asian exited, deep in the conversation. After they had passed, she stepped in and pushed the third-floor button. She tried to recall her events from the previous day, but her mind seemed too swollen with fogginess. All she really remembered was the near panic attack. It was too close.

Inside her condo unit, Jewel dropped her bag onto the floor with a yawn. She pushed the door shut with a foot and slapped the lock into place before she retreated to her bed. The curtains were closed and the place was dark, just the right atmosphere conducive for sleeping. With a sigh, she lowered herself onto the bed and closed her eyes as her body sank into the fluffy sheets. Within minutes, she was unconscious and breathing softly. Her chest rose and fell in a steady rhythm.

The next time she opened her eyes, she was in a hallway, frantically looking for a place to hide with thin wisps of curly brown hair framing her round, young face. Behind her, she could hear the voice of a boy nearing the end of his count. "Ready or not, here I come!"

Excitement filled her chest and she rushed to the door at the end of the hall, turning the knob quickly. She stepped inside without another thought, only to freeze at the row of steps that descended into light. She opened her mouth to speak, but no sound came out. Instead, she heard a gentle whine.

Something pushed her forward, and with a small step of curiosity, a foot slid forward to the edge of the first step. Her left hand touched the side of the corridor, fingertips dusting the side of the wall. It was cold to the touch. She descended down several steps, confused and both perplexed by the constant whine and whimper she heard.

Two steps from the bottom she heard something that froze her throat: A deep grunt. It seemed to echo off the walls and reverberate in her chest. As if she were attached to a string, her body continued to move forward until she stood on the last step. She took another and turned.

She saw her eyes first, bright blue and beautiful surrounded by a frump of blond curls, like an angel in the midst of all the light, laying on a foldable bed pushed against the back wall of the basement. Then the darkness came, a man large, white and terrifying appeared before her. She heard the sound of a zipper—he was adjusting his pants.

She realized the small girl on the bed was crying. Her eyes weren't blue but red. Her cheeks were tear-stained. A sob erupted from her mouth. "Grandpa—no!" With wide eyes, the little girl stood before the old man, frozen in fear as he descended upon her.

Jewel sat up suddenly with a gasp. She was covered in sweat and panted, out of breath. Her mouth was dry like stale bread and hair clung to her neck, face and moist body. From her gut, she could feel her stomach weakening.

Pushing herself from the bed, Jewel rushed to her bathroom. No sooner than she had lifted the seat to the toilet bowl, she began to retch, dry heaving until nothing more than a little bile burned its way over her tongue and into the bowl of clear water.

Sweat piled in beads across her body, sliding down in some places where too much had collected. After several more dry heaves, Jewel moved from the toilet to the sink, coughing scratched at her throat painfully. With effort, she turned the knob for the cold water and immediately rinsed her hands. She didn't feel the cold on her face as she splashed it or see that her entire body shook as a wave of fear and terror swept over her and made her knees weak. She grabbed at the counter the best she could and squeezed her eyes shut until her head stopped spinning.

"Breathe, Jewel. Just breathe," her voice barely croaked. She wasn't sure how much time had passed before she felt like her arms would break at her shoulders. She heard the sound of her electronics humming and buzzing in her home. Opening her eyes took effort. Jewel zeroed in on the dark eyes staring back at her from the glass window. They were crystal clear. Her head no longer swam and her breathing was no longer in choked gasps of air.

At length, she stood and thought back to the dream. She turned suddenly and headed back into her bedroom where she pulled open her dresser and drawers. She had lifted piles of clothes before she remembered her handbag in the living room near the front door. Jewel rushed from her bedroom and spotted the bag on the floor, right where she dropped it. She moved to it quickly and withdrew her small notebook, nearly dumping everything else out the bag in the process.

After her fingers had found a pen inside the bag, Jewel flipped to the most recent entry. She began to write, trying to remember as much as she could from the dream. *The sequence has started again. A little girl playing hide and seek...*

The pen scratched against the fibers of white paper within her journal. Her hand seemed stiff and swollen, making writing difficult, but she pressed on, her penmanship large and sloppy. *She tries to hide within a door but walks downstairs where there is an old, white man...*

Jewel paused, a familiar wave of emotion washing over her body, ripping into her heart as it worked itself over her. She squeezed her eyes shut, trying to ignore the sensation, yet this time, when she closed her eyes, she saw the light blue eyes of the small, white girl. They were wide, frightened. Opening her eyes, Jewel continued to write. *The man has raped his granddaughter, and the kid knows his secret.*

With a deep exhalation of air, Jewel paused. She was near breathless again. She stared back at her writing, the scene from the dream flashing through her mind again in short snippets and shots. She remembered the dim lighting in the hallway, and the cool wall beneath the fingertips of the child.

Jewel grabbed her head, grabbing fistfuls of hair as she squeezed her eyes shut again. Jewel instantly began to cry out to the only one she knew could give her peace in moments like this. " Jesus, Jesus...." she whispered His name over and over. "I need your peace right now. Please help me. Take these thoughts from my mind and give me peace."

After several moments, the scenes stopped evading her mind and she opened her eyes, seeing the ending of the last sentence she had written.

Ringing sounded throughout the still apartment. Jewel jumped at the sound, confused until she realized it was her cell phone. Reaching for it from within her handbag, her heart seized as she saw she had seven missed calls from David.

5

A Relationship in Turmoil

Jewel panicked and looked down at herself. She was still in her work clothes and she just knew her hair was a mess. She began to frantically work her tired fingers through her hair as she looked around the open space of the living room for a mirror. Her mind moved too fast for her to find one. In defeat, she tried to answer the phone. Bringing it to her ear, she waited eagerly for David's voice, as she slipped her shoes on.

With the phone to one ear, and her hand grabbing her bag in the other, she managed to push the lock open with her elbow. In the hallway, Jewel hiked her purse to her shoulder and then pulled the phone down, staring at the screen. It was blank.

She locked her door quickly, nearly breaking the key in the lock as she pulled it out, trying to turn away at the same time. She sprinted to the elevator and jabbed the button for service. While she waited, she tried calling David back. Once she heard her phone begin to ring, she pushed it to her ear and tapped her foot nervously. After two rings, there was finally an answer.

"David, baby, I'm on my way," Jewel said in a rush, out of breath. The doors of the elevator opened slowly and she bounded inside, stabbing for the parking floor.

"You are still coming tonight?" His voice was tense and strained.

"Yes, baby, of course. I'll be there, I promise."

David was silent across the line. After a long pause, Jewel heard his smooth voice once again. "I'll wait another 20 minutes, Jewel."

"Okay, thank you, babe. I'll be there. Getting in the car right now."

Once the elevator doors opened, Jewel ran through the aisles until she located her car by unlocking it remotely. She nearly threw herself into the seat, yanking her seatbelt down and shoving the metal into the lock. Starting the car with the same amount of rush, Jewel forced the car into reverse and began to back out the parking space.

She continued to run her fingers through her hair to thin out the frizz around her face and at the edges. Her shirt was a little damp in areas, but the loose flowing fabric barely made it noticeable. By the time she arrived at the restaurant, she was back into flight mode, rushing through the parking lot, past double doors until she reached the maitre'd.

Before the tall, thin woman could address, Jewel, she pointed past her head. "That's him. I'm his guest," she urged. The woman followed Jewel's finger towards David. His back was to her, but she would have been able to spot his build from any point within the room.

"I'll take you right over," the woman said with a forced smile.

"Thank you." As she was ushered to David's small table, Jewel ran her hands over the top of her hair one last time. She wished she had a chance to check her makeup, but she also knew that would only make her even later. By the time she figured she had received his calls, he had been waiting 30 minutes. The restaurant was 15 minutes from her house.

Jewel chided herself with anger. She had never been this late before. Hesitantly, Jewel reached towards David's shoulders, allowing her fingertips to acknowledge her presence. He looked up. A half-smile crossed his face. In the next moment, he stood, drawing Jewel into his arms.

"I'm glad you made it," he said softly, brown eyes bearing back into hers.

Jewel leaned into him and gave him a quick peck on the lips. David was stiff. When she pulled away, he searched her face intently. "Where have you been?" Jewel blinked. *Don't lie.* In a tuff, she flipped her hair over her shoulder, thinking for a moment to tell him the truth.

"I left the office, but I ended up needing to go back to finish case studies."

As he watched her face, David frowned. He sat down and gestured for Jewel to follow suit. Sitting down, Jewel wiped her palms on top of her thighs. She noticed that the table had only been set for one. Confused, she met David's brown eyes again. He wasn't happy.

"Why didn't you at least answer my calls?" He asked at last. Jewel nodded, wiping a wisp of hair away from her face.

Pressing her lips together, Jewel sighed. "The ringer must have been off so that I could work," she groped for words to say. "I've just been so swamped at work. I was just trying to do everything

I could to get caught up."

Lowering his eyes, David placed a palm on the white table cloth. He examined his hand slowly and then moved it towards the stem of his wine glass. It was filled and bristling with a sparkling wine. He gripped the stem of the glass and brought it to his lips, swallowing several times before he sat it down.

"Are you caught up now?" He asked in an even softer voice.

"What?" Jewel glanced at him, eyes bouncing from David's frame before her to the approaching waiter.

"Wine, Miss?" The waiter asked as he approached the table.

Jewel shook her head, waving a hand at the platter holding an empty glass. "Water," she said quickly and met David's eyes again. Her brow furrowed as she saw his unconvinced face. After the waiter had poured water into a new glass, he bowed out, taking a step back to retreat to another area of the restaurant.

"What did you say?" Jewel asked again.

David watched her carefully, lifting his glass again. "I asked if you had at least caught up."

The question stopped Jewel. Her mind raced for an answer until she realized he was asking about her work. She did have case studies to do, and she was behind on her work. She was nowhere near getting caught up; but, she would have been closer to it if she had actually been in her office working.

"I still have several cases I need to update. Mr. Pierce has asked for them by Friday," with a nod, Jewel lifted the crystal glass before her to her lips. She drank with an uneven hand, holding David's stare for as long as he continued to look at her.

After a while, he shrugged. "Are they understaffed at the center?"

Jewel laughed, shrugging her shoulders. "Yes and...no?" She pulled the water in front of her, holding it around the base with both of her hands. "Look, baby, I know I've let you down," Jewel began.

"What did you think of the flowers?" David asked her suddenly.

Jewel frowned. "Flowers? What—Oh," she laughed and placed a hand on her chest as she remembered the beautiful bouquet from earlier. Landra probably still had them because she forgot to take them with her. "The flowers were absolutely fantastic," with a broad grin, Jewel reached for David's hand across the table.

He didn't stop her, but he didn't move towards her either. At his stiffness, Jewel's smile fell. She searched his face deeply. "David, baby, please."

"Please what?" David asked his brow knotting in between his eyes. "I feel like I'm in this relationship alone, Jewel. You're at least fifteen minutes late to nearly half an hour to every date we make. You ignore most of my calls and barely remember the things I do for you and get you to show you that I'm thinking of you."

Withdrawing her hand, Jewel blinked furiously. She reached for the glass of water and forced her hands around the base. "David, you're not fair," she said softly, her voice degrees softer than before.

David's face softened as he watched her. "Jewel, I don't think *you're* being fair. Tell me what you want out this relationship."

Jewel sniffed and wiped at the side of her face again. Her eyes pleaded eagerly with David's. "I want you. You know that I do."

David shook his head with a frown. "No, Jewel," his eyes jumped across the features of her face. "I don't know that you do. Why do you ignore my calls?"

"I don't ignore them, baby," Jewel entreated, her voice continuing to fail her.

"Well, you don't answer them," David finished for her. "You don't answer my texts either."

Jewel placed a hand on her forehead and pushed against her skin. She felt pressure beneath her temples and her pulsating heartbeat racing through her veins. It was the beginning of a headache for sure.

"Sometimes I just don't have time."

"And what is that supposed to mean?" David asked, lowering his voice considerably as he leaned across the table. "You don't have time to respond to me? A man that's here and trying to be in a relationship with you?"

Jewel searched his eyes. "Please, David. I don't," a tear escaped. She was angrier at herself than anything. Wiping at the tear frantically, Jewel focused on the glass of water before her. She noticed how the condensation beaded along the cup before it slid to the bottom. When she closed her eyes, she saw the blue hues of the small white girl on the fold-away bed. Jewel squeezed the image away and tried to focus on the reality in front of her.

"I don't ignore you," she forced out. "I'm not purposefully late and I don't mean for you to feel this way." Jewel raised her eyes, sniffing again. She reached for his hand with strength, grabbing it despite his lack of enthusiasm.

When David didn't move, she placed her other hand on his. "I'm here," she nodded. "Right here and right now. Can't we try to enjoy this evening together?"

David's frown deepened. He leaned over the table towards her. "Jewel, I'm not here to just enjoy the night," he said it with thick disdain. "You act like this is the first time we've had this conversation. I want to move forward with you, Jewel. I want to have something with you—a future."

With a tired sigh, Jewel removed her hands and brought her palms to her head. She rubbed her temples hard, frequently sighing in heavy exhalations of air. "David," she shook her head, "Why are you trying to rush things?"

"Are you serious?"

With everything she said David seemed to become more and more upset. Jewel removed her hands and sat back in her chair with a scowl. Flinging a hand towards him she said, "We have a good thing, David. Why are you always trying to make it more complicated than it has to be?"

With a chortle, David scoffed. His eyes grew wide as realization dawned on him and he began to shake his head in disbelief. "So that's what this is to you? Me making things complicated?"

Jewel frowned and crossed her arms. "Well, what are you trying to do?"

"Jewel," his voice hardened, "I want a future with you," he said plainly. "I've *wanted* a future with you," he paused, "If that's something you can't give me then let me know right now."

Jewel's frown deepened. She loosened a hand to run it through her hair, trying to hold back a dam of tears. David watched her. He attempted to touch her hand, but Jewel yanked it away and stood abruptly.

"Excuse me," she whispered before rushing towards the bathroom. She had seen the sign on her way in and bristled towards it now, bumping into a standing patron along the way.

She didn't pause to stop. She just held out a hand behind her instead with a simple, "I'm sorry." Inside the bathroom, she enclosed herself in the handicap stall and locked the door. No sooner than the metal locked into place her tears began to fall. Large sobs racked her body. She had never been so forthcoming with David before and she had never seen him so upset.

Attempting to sniff back her tears, Jewel looked towards her leather handbag. She had managed to grab it before she rushed to the bathroom. Now she wondered if David would even still be there by the time she emerged. Digging into the purse for her phone, Jewel found it and quickly selected Landra's phone number. While it dialed, she closed her eyes. After four rings, her heart began to race again, her sobs becoming more audible.

She disconnected the call and tried again. "Come on, Landra. Please, pick up the phone," she whined, counting the rings. She stopped once she reached five. After several more rings, she disconnected the call and lowered her phone into the bag. Pushing her head against the stall door, she closed her eyes again and started practicing a breathing routine she learned many years ago.

She took one deep breath in for every two breaths out. It stretched her lungs and sometimes made her dizzy, but it never failed to calm her hyperventilation down. After the seconds had morphed into minutes, Jewel opened her eyes. She stood tall and smoothed down her clothes.

Unlocking the bathroom stall, Jewel stepped out and moved to the long row of sinks in front of the half glass pane along the entire back wall of the stalls. She looked at her face. Her eyes were still pink from her tears and her cheeks seemed a little swollen. She didn't think David would notice. Wiping the remaining moisture off her cheeks, Jewel took another deep breath and exited the bathroom.

David was still at the table. She crossed the floor of the restaurant much slower than she had traversed it on her way to the bathroom. When she took her seat across from David, his eyes told her that he had taken the time to calm down as well. With a deep breath, Jewel began to speak again.

"David, I don't want to waste your time. I want to be with you," she nodded firmly, believing her voice and its strength. "I love you, David."

David ran his eyes over Jewel's face, his own composure cracking. "Then what is it, Jewel? Why are you doing this to us?"

"I just," Jewel lowered her eyes for a moment before reconnecting them with David's gaze. "I'm going through some things and I need you to be patient, baby."

A flicker of hardness dashed across David's face. "You told me that six months ago, Jewel. Do I need to wait another half a year?"

"Baby," Jewel's voice was hard, but uneven, falling through the spaces of her speech, "please just wait for me. I don't want to lose you, David. I love you." She reached for his hands, gripping them tightly. "Don't question what we have, please. Just give me time. More time, baby," she pleaded, not caring for decency, "I need more time."

She could see the pain on his face. David's muscles tensed

beneath her touch, but he didn't move to hold or touch her back. After a moment, Jewel dropped her head, exasperated. She wondered if telling him the truth would make any difference. If he would stay, call her crazy, or leave.

"I haven't been sleeping too well lately either," Jewel offered. She didn't seek out his eyes, keeping them low. Her body tensed for his next words, cringing in the silence that followed.

"Insomnia?" His voice was gentle. Jewel snapped her eyes to his. Her body relaxed as she saw the concern in his eyes. After a pause, she shook her head.

"No. I fall asleep. I'm just so tired during the day," she shook her head. "I don't stay asleep for more than three or four hours." David's hand twitched beneath her palm. Relaxing her hand, Jewel allowed a weak smile. He moved to cradle her hands instead.

"How long has this been going on?" David stroked the top of one hand with the thick pad of his thumb.

Swallowing, Jewel shook her head. "I don't honestly remember." She sniffed, glancing around them. "It seems to be getting worse," she nearly whispered. "I have trouble getting up. I'm so tired in the morning." David took a long, steady breath. After a moment of hesitation, he tugged on Jewel's hand, pulling her to stand. A playful giggle escaped.

"What are you doing?" Jewel asked. David didn't answer. He continued to tug on her hand, drawing her around the table to stand in front of him where he pulled her into his lap. His touch soothed her mind. Her thoughts ceased as he wrapped his arms around her body, nuzzling his head into her arms.

"When will you let me in?" He pulled away from her slightly. He peered up, searching her soul through her eyes.

Jewel broke their connection and lowered her gaze. She leaned into him, planting a kiss on his forehead. When she pulled away, he lifted his chin up, trying to meet her eyes. Instead, Jewel lowered her head and allowed their lips to connect. She pushed against him and tasted the moist of his mouth. David didn't pull away.

6

Where's Julianna?

"Crisscross applesauce!" Ella called out, her voice ringing throughout the empty space of the living room. Groggy-eyed kids struggled to obey. She heard the small bodies mumbling while others chirped and kicked into high gear as they talked about their upcoming snack.

The children lined up in the usual lines of four kids to a row. Melody, the additional staff member, helped them find their seats. She sat the kids down on a mark on the ground, a sticky little apple that gave them something to interest themselves while they waited for their after nap time snack.

"I want a granola."

"I like the apples."

"Cookies!"

The children's voices mixed and mingled. Some still sagged with the lingering effects of sleep. Ella smirked under her breath. Opening the daycare center was the best decision she and her husband could have ever made. From the kitchen, a room positioned to the left of the living room, Ella could still see the children from the cut out that made serving breakfast, lunch, and afternoon snacks a breeze. She eyed the kids loosely; something seemed off.

"Ms. Ella, where's Julianna?" A small girl called from her spot on an apple. Her legs were spread and she poked at the eyes on the apple mindlessly.

Ella didn't look up. "Probably behind you sweetie."

"But Ms. Ella," the little girl whined.

Before Ella could readdress the child, Melody was at her side with a shaking voice.

"Julianna's not here."

Ella blinked, and then began to turn towards the children. Melody grabbed her attention, reaching for her arm with a tight grip. "Shhhh, look. Don't scare the kids."

Nodding this time, Ella forced her eyes to Melody's face. She saw fear. "Julianna is not here," Melody repeated, her voice a deep, ragged rumble of terror. Her eyes were wide and frantically searched Ella's face.

Swallowing back, Ella took a deep breath. Children went missing inside of houses all the time. "We'll have to look for her then. The kids were playing hide and go seek earlier, remember?" Her tone was soft and calm, soothing the wrinkles of fear from Melody's eyes. "She might still be playing with the other kids."

"And fallen asleep," Melody said with a sigh and a weak nod.

Ella smile. "That's right. Let's ask the kids when they saw Julianna last. We'll tell them she's still playing hide and go seek still."

"But the snack," Melody reminded. She shot a tense glance towards the kids. She couldn't fake a smile.

"Okay, you begin looking. Check the bathrooms," Ella started to wipe her hands on the white apron tied around her waist, "check the closet."

Melody frowned this time. "What would she be doing in the closet?"

Ella raised her brows and straightened her back. "Kids get creative when it's time to hide. Don't call her name. We don't want her to think she's in trouble."

The assistant's breath still wavered. Her body shook with the release of adrenaline. With effort, she lifted her right hand to her face to push her hair aside. "Okay. I'll start looking first." She managed a nod.

Taking a deep breath, Ella smiled. "I'll take care of the snacks."

Melody took two steps back before turning to leave the kitchen. Watching the assistant leave, Ella felt her own throat turning dry. She forced a swallow and faced the kids. Nine pairs of beady eyes looked back at her.

"Ready for your snack?" The children smiled, some squealed, one even jumped up in the excitement, causing two more to start to stand. "No, no. Stay seated and I'll pass out the snack, just like always." Ella exited the kitchen and sought for Melody. She tried to listen for her footsteps, but the sound was drowned out by the children as they began to grab the small plastic plates from her hand. Today, the snacks were apples, crackers, and cheese. Cheese for everyone except Lucas. He was lactose intolerant and received an extra dose of crackers instead.

Grabbing the designated plate for Lucas, Ella grabbed a regular plate in her hand and finished the first row accordingly. She caught Melody's eyes as she came from the activity room, her shoulders hunched up and her arms moved out with an empty, confused shrug. She shook her head for emphasis and then pointed to the staff bathroom across from the kitchen.

Ella mouthed, "Keep looking," and then turned to the children, forcing her smile to grow. Her mind wanted to race, but she kept it silent by engaging the children. "Another plate for Ms. Molly and Michael," the children giggled at the way she wrinkled her nose.

Seconds later, Melody reappeared, her resolve was slipping. Ella mouthed, "Search the backyard." Melody's frown only deepened. It was unlikely the child would be outside.

Ella repeated her order silently, lips moving without a sound. She tacked on a head nod towards the back door through the house for good measure. She hoped the cool, quiet air would help calm Melody down.

"Ms. Ella, what's Melody doing?" Joshua asked. He chewed loudly. Bits of apple that had escaped the gnashing of his teeth rested on his small, plump lips.

"She's looking for Julianna," it was the same little girl from earlier, Rose. She was four and very smart. Something Ella usually loved about the girl, except for today.

"She went outside to get some air, child," Ella quipped, eyes glinting at the small, brown girl. Rose shrugged her shoulders and redirected her attention to the apple on her place. A rush of heat spread over Ella as Melody entered from the outside. She didn't try shrugging her shoulders or mouthing anything. Instead, she spoke out loud.

"She's not outside."

"Who's not outside?" A little boy asked.

"I don't want to go outside," another kid whined.

"Julianna," Rose called out. She stood this time, looking around. "Where's Julianna, Ms. Ella?"

Other children began to squirm. Their eyes widened as they realized Rose was right. They began to ask the same question.

"I don't know," Ms. Ella said loudly. She shot Melody a glance with hard eyes before looking back at the kids. She placed her hands on her knees and leaned forward. "Julianna is still playing hide and seek. I need your help, but after snack time, okay?" Some children answered softly while others yelled a response. They were eager to play a game.

"Rose, can you take your seat again dear?" The rush of anger subsided as Rose calmed down. She saw now that concern was plastered on the little girl's face. Julianna and Rose were best friends at the center. They entertained each other, sat next to each other, and even wanted to sleep next to each other when it was naptime. "You can help me find Julianna after snack time."

From her peripheral vision, Ella saw Melody motioning for her to join her. After another comforting smile, Ella excused herself from the children to join Melody in the front room closest to the front door.

"You're going to need to keep your calm," Ella said with a low, stern voice.

Melody's eyes pleaded a different case. "We need to report this now."

"Report what?" Ella asked, her brow deepening. "The police will ask if we've searched the house. That's what we need to do first," Ella glanced towards the children. Her offer to include them in the search had calmed them down.

"Please try not to scare them. When it's time to call the police, we will," she gave a firm nod, "Okay? I'm sure Julianna fell asleep hiding." Ella looked around herself. She felt a gnawing on her soul. "Five more minutes with the snacks," she called out.

The children were ready within a couple minutes to move. Only a few remembered that Julianna was missing and Rose helped them to remember, jumping up minutes into the five-minute time limit to ask again about Julianna. Ella cursed beneath her breath. Rose should have been removed. Maybe then the rest of the children would forget for the time being.

"Are we going to look for Julianna now?" Leroy asked. He was a little heavier set, a fluffy dark-skinned boy with waves in his hair. Ella clasped her hands together and nodded. Gesturing towards Melody, she whispered, "Can you move Rose to the front room? Keep her there. We can distract the kids for a while and then redirect them to a movie or something," her thoughts were starting to scatter. She wondered where Alan was.

Melody moved quickly, her bright smile and high-pitched voice convinced Rose to follow her into the adjacent room. The two couldn't be left alone, but Ella didn't know what else to do. She gathered the rest of the children and had them begin searching the room they were in. They giggled and looked beneath their sticky apples, knowing Julianna couldn't be beneath them. She moved them to the activity room and directed them to search the bins with toys. They could help her pick them up later, or she would do it once this whole mess was sorted out. At the moment, it didn't matter. She searched the tall, smart storage cabinets. They could hide children, but they hid no one and stored assorted equipment and paraphilia for the daycare.

The hallway towards the home office and bedrooms had been blocked off with a baby gate. She'd have to look back there. With a quick search for Melody, she found the young assistant bringing Rose with her.

"Can you get a movie started for the kids in the living room? Keep the activity room open for those that aren't interested." Ella's voice was strained.

"What are you going to do?" Melody asked in a hushed whisper.

Ella blinked. Her mouth was dry. She glanced towards Rose and squatted. "You're worried for Julianna aren't you?" Rose nodded; her eyes were full and light brown. "She's going to be okay," Ella nodded. She wasn't sure if it was okay to promise such a thing, but the young girl needed to believe that her best friend was okay. "Julianna wasn't feeling well today."

"She was fine while we played hide and go seek, Ms. Ella," Rose contended. She had long straight hair, brown and full in stark contrast to the head of hair on her missing best friend.

"I know," Ms. Ella nodded. "We're going to call Julianna's mommy and daddy. They'll find her. I think she's sleeping."

Rose studied Ella's face. Her lips slowly curled into a smile. With a reassuring nod, Ella rubbed the small child's back. "Do you want to watch a movie or do an activity?"

"Movie," Rose said quickly. Ella moved to the side and watched Rose run to the small group of children who had gathered for the film. The rest waited restlessly in the activity room. They pulled out the toys and two were in the process of emptying the arts and crafts bin of crayons and colored pencils. She forced a sighed and looked to Melody. The assistant saw the waiting mess and nodded.

"I'll start the movie and keep them busy," she met Ella's eyes with confusion and terror. "What are you going to do?"

"I need to check the bedrooms and the hidden bathroom in the back. If she's not there, we'll have to call the parents and then the police."

7

Missing

A car swerved to a stop haphazardly at the curb of the daycare. The two officers standing on the lawn looked up before springing into action.

"Remove Ms. Fuller to the inside, I've got the mother."

"Julianna!" A tall, cream-colored woman with blonde hair was out the car before the ignition was cut. "Where's my baby?" She shouted, head swiveling from the left and right. Her eyes narrowed on Ella being ushered into the interior of the house. She pointed a finger and began to sprint, shouting, "Where's Julianna? Julianna!"

An officer had caught her around the waist before she made it to the house. Ella's eyes were wide with fright as she disappeared into the home.

"Ma'am, we're going to need you to calm down," the officer

said, gently restraining the lanky woman. "Are you Sandy? Julianna's mom?" The woman still screamed and shouted. Her body grew limp in the officer's arms as her energy drained and her voice became hoarse.

A darker man emerged from the car. His eyes scanned the scene on the lawn of the house and then he moved to Sandy's side. He took her into her arms and she collapsed into crying.

"I'm William, Julianna's father, and Sandy's husband," his voice was aged and sharp with authority. He glared at the officer who had previously held his wife. "Can someone tell me what's going on here? Where's Julianna? Where's my daughter?"

The officer straightened himself before William as he cleared his throat. William was a tall, well-built black man that stood several inches above the officer. With a scratchy voice, the officer began to speak. "Your daughter was reported missing from the center shortly after the naptime schedule."

Upon hearing the officer confirm what she had been told over the phone, Sandy's cries erupted as she screamed, "No! Julianna!"

William held her tightly in his arms. He cradled her head into the nook of his shoulder and scanned the lawn again. "How is this possible?" He spoke through clenched teeth. The muscles in his arm twitched. "How do you lose a child?"

Melody stood at the door of the home. She watched the parents question the officer before she stepped forward. She didn't speak loudly, but when she did, William listened. "The kids were playing hide and go seek before naptime. Ms. Ella was in the office while I was with the kids," her face was wet with tears. William's face only hardened. "I laid them all down but was busy handling one of our more difficult sleepers, Matthew. When it was time for snacks, we noticed she was missing." Her body began to shake as a sob escaped. "I'm so sorry."

The officer standing in between them motioned for Melody to say no more. He turned to William and spoke softly. "It's likely that your daughter went missing during the last game before nap time. With the limited supervision, it's possible she could have slipped away undetected."

"We thought she was still hiding and had just fallen asleep," Melody said with a gasp.

William breathed heavily through his nose. His jaw tightened, clenched to the point where he could no longer speak. He maintained his eyesight with the officer. "Where's my baby?" It was more of a demand than a question.

"When was the last time you saw her?" The officer asked, turning to Melody.

She sniffed and wiped at her face. She struggled to recall. "I was in the activity room and Ms. Ella was watching them play. She told me she needed to make a fax." The young woman spoke quickly, with words tumbling out of her mouth so fast the officer had to direct her to slow down several times. They were only supposed to use the living room and the snack room they take naps in, but there isn't much they could hide behind."

William's eyes snapped to the front door as Ms. Ella emerged. There was an older man at her side who he had never seen before. He wore slacks and tucked in pastel covered shirt. Their eyes snagged and held. "Who are you?" William demanded. The officer turned to eye the man quickly.

"Alan Fuller. Ms. Fuller's husband," he answered quickly.

William took a step forward, causing Sandy to stand and turn with him. Her small, pencil eyes looked over Alan.

"Where's my daughter?" She questioned.

Something flickered across Alan's face. He looked William and Sandy over and then flashed his eyes towards the officer. "Are we done here?" His voice was a low rumble, but from the distance Sandy and William stood with the officer in between them, he could tell there was anger.

"Are we done here?" William challenged. He released his wife and squared himself to address Alan thoroughly. "We'll be done when my daughter is found."

A police officer emerged from the side of the house. He began to motion towards the officer standing in between Julianna's parents and the daycare owners. "The door leading to the basement is locked," the officer near the gate spoke. He pulled the speaker of his radio into his collar and then repeated the message. He paused briefly, scanning the faces of William and Sandy before he began to grow red. He let the radio microphone drop back to his shirt and angrily pointed to the road. "Who told them to come here?"

At the curb, two vehicles rolled to a stop. One was the local news station's live broadcast van and the other was a small, blue sedan. There were shouts and orders from the officers and a blur of movement. The officer in the sidewalk between Julianna's parents and the owners quickly ushered William and Sandy onto the green lawn in front of the home's large windows. The officer that had emerged from the back moved to greet the media, a man with a high-tech shoulder broadcast camera with another holding a mic stand. A younger woman was told not to move from her vehicle. She didn't listen and ran to join at her camera crew's side.

The officer's tone was harsher with them. He wouldn't let them pass. Alan started to shout, "Get them out of here!" Melody and Ella were escorted back inside.

"Sir!" The woman to emerge from the sedan had brown hair. She waved her arms to get William's attention. "Are you the parents of the little girl that went missing?" The reporter yelled across the lawn.

The officer who had directed Julianna's parents attempted to intervene, but William spoke over him loudly. When Sandy saw the reporter, she dashed across the lawn to speak with the woman. The officer swore. He turned to speak to William, but the large man held up a hand before moving to join with his wife.

"Who called them here?" An officer shouted.

"I did," William snapped, looking for the voice. He met a body of hard faces and glares from the officers. "I need this whole neighborhood looking for my baby girl," he turned to join his wife.

"How long has your daughter been enrolled with this daycare?" The reporter began, directing the filming crew with her eyes and hands. She held the microphone instinctively towards Sandy whose face was still streaked with the last tears she cried.

"I've never heard of anything happening like this before," she began after a deep intake of air. She glanced behind her towards the officers. They had joined near the door with the owners and watched on in disgust. "I just want my baby. Nobody's telling us anything," she pleaded with the camera.

At the door of the house, Alan snarled. "Can you get that crew off our porch?"

The two cops turned to him but didn't answer. A third emerged from the house, but only made eye contact with Ella. "We need to get into one of the rooms back here. It's locked."

Ella frowned. "What are you talking about?"

"There's a room we need to search," the officer repeated. His voice was hard, but he repeated himself slowly, looking over Ella's confused face and Allan's scorned grimace. "I need you to unlock it, please."

"I'll go," Allan answered with a sneer. He left Ella's side and disappeared into the house. Ella wringed her hands and turned to watch the reporter greedily interview the parents of one of her favorite children. She was aware this would likely result in a loss of business. At this moment, all she could think about was where Julianna could be.

She had searched the rooms and any place she could think of twice. Nothing made sense. There was no way Julianna could have "escaped". Why would she leave? Her thoughts were put on hold as an officer's voice began to ring from the radio attached to one of the officer's uniform.

"We have a small puddle of liquid down here in the basement," the voice announced.

Ella's hands were on her chest. She clawed at them nervously, having heard the information. It made her frown. She didn't understand why they would be in the basement. It was always locked.

"Test it," the officer responded. The one who spoke wore a badge that read Herrington. Ella looked the letters over before finding her voice to speak.

"The basement is locked during the day," she paused and

spoke again as if an afterthought, "It's always locked, actually."

"It's urine," the voice crackled through the radio. Officer Herrington turned the volume down and looked towards Ella again.

"Always locked?" He asked. She nodded. His face flicked to unreadable. He took several steps back before turning to head towards the side of the house, towards the backyard. As he turned, Ella saw him speaking into the microphone. Her gut twisted and coiled in a way that made her want to puke.

"Are you okay?" The other officer spoke. He reached for Ella as her knees gave way beneath her. He caught her moments before her knees crashed into the floor.

8

Honored Guest

Jewel smoothed the fabric of her black dress down. Sequins glistened in the mirror, swirling across her bust in the sleeveless lace-backed long gown. She felt elegant with the soft, silky fabric bristling against her skin. Glancing towards the thin-banded watch wrapped around her wrist, she took a deep breath. David would be arriving within ten minutes. She didn't want him to wait and worry about whether or not she'd answer his call.

Exiting the bathroom, Jewel reached for her matching clutch resting on the covers of her bed. She eyed her journal and paused. She wanted to review the notes she had been writing, the dreams, but she forced herself away from the thought. She needed to focus only on the evening. Jewel forced out a breath of air and closed her eyes, taking another deep breath. She counted down mentally from ten to one with each pass of air. One in, two out. Her heart slowed.

A bit of anxiety bubbled within her, but as she reached one, it had dissolved and dissipated. She opened her eyes and smiled. "Showtime."

She exited her room leisurely and strolled towards the elevator shaft at the end of the hall. On the ground floor, she pushed through the doors to wait outside the building. Within minutes, David rolled to a stop through the rounded drive through. His face beamed as he saw Jewel waiting. He opened his mouth to say something, but Jewel spoke first as she skipped to the side of the door.

"You see? You're important to me," she leaned through the window and pulled him into a kiss. She felt his lips smiling against hers.

"We better get going," David said after a pause. Jewel pulled away and searched his twinkling eyes. He looked her over, the smile fading momentarily as his face solidified. "You look absolutely incredible," he said in a breath, meeting Jewel's eyes. She smiled, hands resting on the rim of the window.

David wore a plain suit, a Vice President, and branch manager of the Chase on the corner of Madison and Wabash. He placed a hand on the door. Jewel moved her hand to cover his, their eyes never breaking contact.

"You look pretty incredible yourself," she offered with a smile. David ran his eyes over her face and upper torso one more time and then pulled her into him for another, deeper kiss. She felt his desire, his need. His passion took her breath away. When he pulled away this time, she was a step from breathless.

Jewel tried clearing her throat to welcome air into her lungs. David chuckled. "We better get going," he repeated. Jewel nodded, moving around the front of the vehicle to let herself into the passenger seat.

The CARE awards dinner was being held at the Ravenswood Event Center, an incredible event space that had once been reserved for making advertising billboards in the downtown area of the city. The floor was covered with waxed wood and timber beams with the walls fashioned from massive wall to floor glass windows and old century style brick.

Inside the loft of the event center, David and Jewel found seating among the other staff of the private therapist and counseling group. Landra sat with Mr. Pierce, his wife, and Ronald at her right. She gladly welcomed Jewel and David to her left.

Water glasses were filled and pitchers of water and plain tea sat in the middle of the table. Jewel quickly helped herself to the unsweetened tea. David rested a large hand on her back and rubbed gently, up to her shoulders and then down to her lower back. Jewel caught Ronald's eyes for a moment before he turned and eyed her date. David didn't seem to notice and leaned towards Jewel, kissing the nip of her shoulder.

Grinning, Jewel turned towards David. Her lips spread into a full smile. She had never thought it would be possible to find a man like him within her lifetime. Everything about him, from the security he brought from his job to the love he carried for Jewel into the relationship, he was truly a catch. Some days, Jewel couldn't even believe that she had been able to catch his eye.

"Ladies and gentlemen, honored guests and therapists," there was a pause. The light conversation quieted to near nonexistent and Jewel turned her attention towards the makeshift stage at the front of the room. "Welcome to our annual C.A.R.E. Awards ceremony." The room erupted into applause and the speaker, a tall, thin middle-aged man in a navy blue suit hovered over a mic attached to a podium.

"We are here tonight, ladies and gentleman, to honor some very, *very* special people." The more the man spoke, the smoother his voice became. He removed the microphone from the holder and began to pace the floor. His left hand moved freely and added enforcement to every emphasized word he spoke. "People who have worked diligently to give outstanding and invaluable service to the community," the announcer paused, eyes scanning the room, "and ultimately the clients they serve."

The announcer continued his speech. He was the president of the group that housed the firm she worked for. They had won numerous contracts with the state, but also held an impressive number of private schools who outsourced the needs of their children to the center.

Landra caught Jewel's attention with a head nod. Turning towards her friend, Jewel felt comforting warmth spread over her body. Landra was dressed for the semi-formal event, wearing a thin-strapped long sheer gown with a stitched floral pattern decorating her bust and moving down the side stretch of fabric. She had always been the type of woman to understate her appearance and wore a thin layer of blush and concealer. Landra reached for Jewel's hand and gave a gentle squeeze. Jewel smiled brightly before turning her attention back to the announcer.

"The first on our list of individuals to honor is a therapist who has consistently shown her dedication and commitment to her job over the years to help find breakthrough for the toughest of clients." Patrons in the room began to nod their heads and curiously look about. "They have gone above the call of duty. Their drive can only be described as one from which genuine care and concern and belief in the good difference they can make in the lives of others comes from," the words echoed and ricocheted off the old brick within the room. Jewel felt her stomach tighten.

"They have repeatedly answered the call and have striven for the utmost of excellence in doing so," the man's eyes scanned the room. His eyes seemed to fall on Jewel's table. He took in the faces seated at her table slowly.

"Out of a consistent case load of 20 to upwards of at most *even* 30 individuals at a time," the man chuckled. His eyes moved to Ronald and quickly passed to Landra, "They have successfully closed cases and over the course of the past year have administered to more than 50 clients extensive trauma therapy that has enabled them to return to a normal, healthy standard of living." A few claps started to ring throughout the room, only to stop as the announcer lifted a palm to indicate he wasn't finished. His eyes passed from Landra to Jewel and settled.

"She has never stopped providing incredible care to her clients," a brief pause, "Ladies and gentlemen, please rise and help me extend the greatest of honors to Ms. Jewel Kennedy."

Landra's head snapped towards her friend. Jewel's mouth was agape, the corners of her lips tight. She blinked, the sound seeming to disappear from around her. It was several seconds before she realized everyone at her table was staring at her with large smiles. They clapped and urged her to stand. Jewel looked towards David. He wore pride and nodded towards the stage.

"That's my girl," he said softly.

Jewel stood finally, making eye contact with Landra for a brief moment. Her eyes skipped Ronald and passed to land on Mr.

Pierce before she turned to the sea of smiling faces and clapping bodies making a way for her to reach the stage. She acknowledged the applause with a hand while she walked. She briefly caught faces as she made her way to the podium. The announcer gave her a glass statue after he set the microphone on the podium. She took the statue in stride and continued to the wooden post. Once there, she turned to face the audience.

The applause died down, the lights shining on her dimmed and faces became slightly recognizable. After a moment to swallow her breath, Jewel leaned into the microphone. "Wow," she laughed, easing the tension in the room with the guests. "This is an incredible honor and right now, I'm completely at a loss for words."

Applause erupted again. Jewel took the moment to make eye contact with the announcer. He smiled and nodded towards the podium, urging Jewel to say more. Clearing her throat, Jewel took a deep breath and attempted to search the faces of the audience.

Counseling and intensive therapy were all she had ever known she wanted to do. To her, it wasn't about the awards or recognition, but about the healing she could help bring to women, young and old. She wanted to help them achieve acceptance through information and support. She identified with each woman that came to her, from a spouse who had suffered harsh domestic violence and marital rape for years to little children who had been robbed of their innocence due to forced incest.

All of her patients had one thing in common when they came to her for help: a sincere belief that they were worthless. With her counseling, she had been able to help many women return to live normal lives. She helped break barriers that prevented them from having deep, intimate relationships and helped them discover happiness. Seeing that type of healing made the long hours at her job worth it.

The pain she dealt with—the absolute horrors of knowing about the most disgusting activities she could imagine were taking place at any given moment in time, and often to the most innocent, during any day only fueled the passion she had for her current list of clients. When she was able to see the progress her clients had made first hand, it breathed life into her she could have never imagined.

Jewel wiped her hands on her dress before placing them on the podium. The applause had died down seconds before and now eyes stared back at her, watching and waiting. Jewel's eyes dropped from the audience to the podium. She noticed the grain of the wood. It had a smooth, flat surface. She eyed the meticulously carved glass statue, the graven image of a large body encircling a smaller figure and cleared her throat again.

"This award is incredible," she began. Jewel looked towards the seated faces of other therapists. She scanned the audience as she spoke. "I am truly humbled and honored," she paused, "I'm thrilled that my work has been noticed and has touched people to the point where they felt like I needed to be recognized," she smiled, allowing herself a chuckle. The audience eased.

"As children, I think it's normal for everyone to feel at one point like they want to change the world," Jewel glanced down momentarily. "You know, that superhero feeling," she pressed her lips together, deep in thought. "Women get it to. That's why we're in politics, in the ER," she looked up. "Women want to save lives. We want to *change* lives." Taking a deep breath, she straightened her back.

"That's why I'm a therapist. I saw that I could do that by helping women heal," she gestured towards her table near the back of the room. "I work alongside some of the most incredibly amazing individuals," she caught Ronald's and Landra's eyes. "They work tirelessly at my side to help restore lives that have been broken by the most dejected realities of humanity, just like me."

Jewel sniffed and moved the microphone from the holder. She made brief eye contact with the announcer again and turned to readdress the audience. "It has become my fervent prayer every night that God would use me to make a difference," she smiled and panned the room. "I hope you will partner with me in the goal of that prayer." She lifted the statue, glancing at it momentarily. "To healing those that are broken," she faced the audience. "Thank you again for honoring the work that I've done and will continue to do."

The room roared to life. Jewel handed off the microphone as she left the stage. Several individuals stopped her on the way to her table, shaking her hand and touching her lightly on the back. Jewel's face beamed as she caught eyes with David first, and then the rest of the members from her table. She caught Ronald's gaze. He smiled sheepishly and glanced towards David, before letting his own eyes fall. At length, she met the gaze of Mr. Pierce and his wife. She gawked.

"Why didn't you tell me you had nominated me for this?" Her tone was mocking, yet playful. Mr. Pierce only offered her a smile in return. "You're one of the hardest workers at our center.

Ronald nodded, finally speaking directly towards Jewel, "You deserve it, Jewel. You're an incredible woman."

David grinned. "Isn't she?" His eyes danced with Jewel's as he looked at her. He extended a hand as she neared him and drew her gently to her chair, but not before he kissed her politely on the cheek. "I still can't believe she's mine."

Mr. Pierce and Landra smiled in agreement. It was soon announced that the food would be served before the listing of the next award was given. Jewel grinned. She caught Ronald's eyes. He watched her silently before suddenly interesting himself with his glass of water. He turned partly in his seat, turning his back towards Landra. Jewel shivered as David ran his hands along the length of her back. She grinned and turned towards him. He smiled back.

"Thank you for supporting me," she whispered.

David's eyes sparkled. "You're an incredible woman, Jewel," he paused. His smile faded slightly. "Don't ever forget it, okay?" He stroked the side of her face briefly and then allowed himself to be pulled into conversation with Mr. Pierce across the table. In the next few moments, waiters and waitresses began to flood the event floor with trays of food. Jewel smiled. Her eyes locked with Landra's.

"What an incredible speech," Landra spoke. She reached for her friend's hand and gave a gentle squeeze. "How are you feeling tonight?"

Jewel chuckled and shrugged her shoulders. "Like I'm in some sort of fairytale."

Landra smiled. "If anyone deserves a happily ever after," she searched Jewel's eyes, "it's you."

The words made Jewel blush. She lowered her eyes and took a deep breath before meeting Landra's gaze again. "Thank you, Landra." Her friend reached towards her and patted her hand.

The lights were still dim and weak. Soft background music

played just beneath the hum of the award patrons and guests. Still, an audible rumble pierced through the chatter and registered in Jewel's ears. She placed an elbow on the table and tried to inconspicuously massage at her temples. The noise grew to a buzz and then a thick hum.

"Do you hear that?" Jewel asked, whispering to David.

He turned to her. His face immediately morphed into concern. "Are you okay?" He touched her shoulder, pushing soft curls from her face. Jewel forced her eyes closed. In the distance, she heard shouting. Someone was angry, furious. Jewel frowned again and pushed herself to stand. Mr. Pierce turned to her, concern taking the place of what was joy only moments before.

"Jewel, what's wrong?"

"Are you okay?" Ronald and Landra looked towards Jewel.

"I'm fine. I need to go to the bathroom," she said softly.

"I'll help," David stood, placing a firm hand on Jewel's lower back. They navigated through the tables and towards the bathroom. Once inside the decorative bathroom, Jewel stopped at the sink to wet her face. She had broken out into a sweat and her hand shook with adrenaline. Her vision began to fade. She barely made it to the soft cushioned pink love seat before the vision overtook her.

She felt devoid of any feelings other than something that tugged at her gut and twisted, pulling and yanking at her from the inside out. Her entire body shook uncontrollably. There was darkness all around her and her voice seemed to have been turned off. Several times she tried to speak, to yell or scream—anything, but no sound came out. Only tears trickled down her face.

There was something hard beneath her. It was cold and comfortless. The room seemed cold and bare, but it was nothing compared to the raw fear hollowing out her insides. She heard a sound, like metal twisting and a door opening. There wasn't a voice, just the scuffling of small feet on the floor.

Seconds later, the door closed, clicking shut. She could hear her breath in the room, fast, sharp and raspsy. She heard a sound and felt a touch on her back, a soft, "Shhhh, it's going to be okay." The voice of a little girl—the one from the bed.

Her stomach convulsed and she gasped for air, her breaths quickening. "Calm down, like this." The young girl worked with her in the dark to calm her rapid hyperventilation. Even in the dark, the room seemed to swirl and paint dots before her closed eyes.

Eventually, the dots stopped swirling before her mind and the darkness of the room stopped dancing with a nauseating spin. She blinked. There was darkness everywhere. She didn't know how it could be so dark. She couldn't tell the difference when her eyes were open or shut. She only knew that they were open because she opened them. She stretched out a hand and touched something soft.

"I'm still here," a girl whispered back. "I have a sandwich. Are you hungry?"

"Wa," she found her voice, a dry crackle of a squeak. She tried again, "Wa-ter," hard syllables as if she had never spoken before.

"I have water," the young girl answered. There was a moment before she heard a snap. She felt the groping hands of the other girl in the darkness with her. A bottle pushed into her face. "Drink," she guided. The girl helped her find her mouth.

The water was so cold, it shocked her. It fell out the sides of her mouth until she remembered to swallow. The liquid chewed its way down her throat, feeling like deliverance, hope, and damnation all at once.

"Food," she managed after the water was pulled away. More groping, more directing and leading until something hard was pushed into her mouth. It caved beneath her teeth and began to dissolve. She couldn't taste whatever it was, but she trusted it was a sandwich, as the little girl told her.

After the bite, she blinked and looked around again. Out of the darkness, anything could come. She timidly whispered, "Mommy?" It was a soft call into the void that could become her hope. She tried again, "Mommy?" Her voice whined. She heard cooing from the girl.

"No. It's just me. Samantha."

9

One Day at a Time

"I don't know what to do," Sandy spoke first from the passenger side of the van. William sat behind the steering wheel. He didn't look towards his wife. With a sharp jerk of movement, he removed the keys and slipped them into his pocket. His eyes were on the door of the front home. "Why did you call the news channel?" Sandy asked at last.

Her husband glanced towards her once before turning to give her full attention. "You think those cops really care about a little black girl gone missing?" He didn't seem to want Sandy to answer. He looked back towards the door to the house. "I don't trust cops," he said with a gruff.

Sandy followed his eyes. The shades and curtains were drawn shut, but she could tell the lights were still on. She thought she heard the TV too. Under normal circumstances, she would have wanted the babysitter to put Keith to bed. Today, however, they assured that if they weren't back before the sun went down, to let him watch movies. They wanted him to be awake when they returned. Now she wasn't so sure that was a good idea. How were they going to get him to sleep?

"We should have let him sleep," she moaned out loud.

William glanced towards her. "We're going to get our baby back," he said with a steady tone. When Sandy didn't turn towards him, he reached for her face and gently took her flesh into his hands. He turned her head and then leaned in to give her a kiss. He wrapped his arms around her body. His warmth and closeness soothed Sandy's soul.

"We're going to get through this," he said with assurance. Sandy pulled away slightly to meet his eyes. He was a good man, a strong man. He sounded like he knew the future, like he had been to tomorrow and knew the secrets it held. Had he found Julianna in the day to come? Sandy searched his face. Would her little girl be safe?

"One day at a time, okay?" He stroked her face. It wasn't a question.

William turned his attention towards the front door and began to unlock his seatbelt. "Let's go." He exited the car first, sure and steady. Sandy moved after he shut the door. She fumbled with the seat belt; her hands and body shook. She thought her mind would race with thoughts, but only one kept coming to her again and again: *Little girls go missing all the time.*

She didn't force herself to catch up with her husband, although he walked significantly slower than usual. At the front door, Sandy could tell that a Disney movie played in the background. The name eluded her, but the music and speech sounded familiar.

William knocked on the door. He rapped twice before they

heard movement inside. The door knob jiggled and a young woman answered. Her eyes widened and she quickly glanced towards the light brown kid on the floor. "Why are you knocking? Everything okay?"

Sandy felt the tears wet on her face again. She couldn't speak. William answered by nodding his head. "They can't find Julianna," he whispered. A hand flew to the young woman's mouth. She instinctively glanced towards the kid on the ground again before stepping outside. She faced Sandy and immediately took the woman into her arms.

"I am so sorry, Ms. Sandy."

"What have you told Keith?"

The babysitter took a step back with one leg to address William. "What you said, that you were going to get his sister."

William looked through the door and nodded. He made eye contact with Sandy and then pulled out his wallet.

"It's okay. Just let me know how I can be of help. I'll watch him however long you need until you can find her," she nodded eagerly.

William paused, but then pulled out a twenty. "We'll call you if we need you, but we'll pay for your help too," he nodded firmly. "Thank you, Deedra."

The babysitter took the money and slipped it into her pocket. She turned back to Sandy. "I'm so sorry for your loss."

"Not yet," William said. His tone was harsh and angry, commanding Deedra's eyes to reconnect with his own. He forced a calm over himself. "She's not lost yet," his voice was much softer.

Deedra nodded. She glanced at the two parents and then she squeezed through them to make her leave. William waited until Sandy had finished wiping her tears before he pushed the door open. Sandy closed it behind them. They stood at the doorway and waited. After a few seconds, the young boy glanced behind him. When he saw his parents, he immediately jumped up, smiling. It faded quickly when he saw their faces. His eyes traveled down their bodies, and then he began to look around.

"Where's Julianna?"

10

Secrets

Several minutes had passed before Jewel realized she was staring into the eyes of Landra. She blinked several times and glanced around her. She still wore the evening gown and was lying on the loveseat in the bathroom. There was another woman behind Landra, who withdrew something from beneath Jewel's nose.

"Smelling salts," said the short, plump woman to the right of Landra. "I'm a physician. A woman found you passed out in the bathroom," she forced a chuckle. "Guess you're not as good with crowds as you looked on stage," she offered.

Jewel sat up, her chest expanding as she took a deep breath of air. She noticed the buzzing and hum in her head had disappeared. She no longer heard shouting. She blinked. "Is the ceremony over?"

The two women before her shook her head. "You've been gone

about ten minutes."

Jewel ran a hand through her hair. Her body tingled like it was jumping, aching for a release of some kind.

"Does this happen often?" The physician asked. Jewel glanced between the two women. Landra was squatting before Jewel, no longer level with her eyes as she was while she had been lying down.

"No," Jewel shook her head and avoided Landra's eyes. "I had a headache and came in here to wash my face."

Landra watched Jewel carefully before she stood and faced the shorter woman. "She has had a couple of dizzy spells before." Jewel winced at Landra's words.

The physician's face changed. She looked down towards Jewel. "Have you been to the doctor about this?"

"Yes."

"No," Landra said harshly, looking down at Jewel.

The physician squatted before Jewel and looked at her more carefully. "Can you look to the left?" Jewel obliged with a heavy sigh. "To the right?" After a moment, the large woman stood with a puff of air. She wiped the back of her hand across her forehead. "Does your friend have a history of high blood pressure?" She asked in a soft whisper. Jewel frowned. Landra shook her head.

The stout woman looked to Jewel, speaking directly to her this time. "If you've had fainting spells before, I can only recommend that you make an appointment with a doctor right away," she paused, "It could be a neurological issue or a symptom of something greater."

Jewel nodded. After a moment, she dropped her eyes. "I can call and make an appointment tomorrow."

Relief spread on the physician's face. "Alright, I've got to get back to my table," she breathed and smiled. "What an excellent speech, by the way," she waited until Jewel met her eyes. "I've read about your work. Just incredible."

Jewel tried to smile. "Thank you." Once the woman exited the bathroom, Jewel met Landra's eyes.

"You've got to stop lying," Landra said with a thin voice. Jewel nodded weakly.

"This is getting out of hand," she answered. She felt cold suddenly and like she didn't belong. "I want to go home," she moaned. Landra pulled her into an embrace. The happiness she had felt just moments before at David's side was gone. If she could, she would simply leave the bathroom and head straight home, but she remembered she didn't drive herself, and her clutch was still resting in her chair beside her date.

"Have you told David?" Landra asked, locking hair behind her ear. She sat down with Jewel and exhaled heavily.

Jewel shook her head. "I don't know how," she answered in a whisper.

Ella clasped her hands as she paced the kitchen floor. They had suspended their services for the next few days. They hadn't told the families that a child went missing, but she was sure they'd find out on the nine o'clock news. Somewhere, she wanted to have anger. Instead, she only felt fear and confusion.

She didn't venture down into the basement. That was Alan's

space. She couldn't explain the urine spot to the cops when they questioned her about it and Alan's blank stare didn't seem to be something they liked either. She didn't know where it would have come from. Did Alan have a weak bladder? Perhaps that would explain why he was rigid with the cops. That sort of thing was embarrassing, but they were only fifty. That was much too young for incontinence, wasn't it?

During the day, the door to the basement had been locked. It was always locked, which is why she didn't think to look down there. Ella looked towards her husband standing by the blinds of the house. She frowned.

"Have you ever left the basement door unlocked?"

She saw Alan's body stiffen. He turned to her, tilting in his head. "What did you say?"

"The basement. An officer asked if children have ever been down there."

His eyes seemed to gloss over and he shook his head. "Door's always locked."

"That's what I thought," Ella looked down and put a finger to her mouth. She chewed absently.

"Think you're a detective, do you?" His tone was too harsh to be playful. Ella frowned.

"Alan, a little girl is missing."

"What do you want me to do about it?" He snapped back. Ella froze at the sudden outburst of anger. She tried to speak, but no words or sounds managed to form. Alan shook his head and grumbled. He faced the blinds and slowly pulled the shades down. Across the street, at the end of the block two houses down, the same unmarked car sat. It had been there since the last parent had arrived to pick up their child. He released the horizontal shades on the blinds quickly and stepped away from the window.

He turned and caught his wife's eye. She watched him silently. With a scowl, he snarled, "What are you looking at?" After a pause, he turned, "I'll be upstairs."

"There she is," Mr. Pierce announced as Jewel neared the table. David turned to meet her. The smile he wore at first faded.

"Everything okay?" David asked, looking from Jewel to Landra. Both women nodded.

"Being on the platform in front of everyone must have done a number on me," Jewel offered with a smile. The table seemed to relax visibly. David stayed focused on Jewel. He held out a hand and helped her to her seat while Landra took her place again next to Ronald.

Their food had arrived while she was in the bathroom. Ronald, Mr. Pierce, and his wife had begun eating. He engaged Landra in soft small talk.

"Baby, you don't look too good," David said in a soft whisper. "Do you need to go home?"

Jewel looked towards David quickly. It was like he could read her mind—she wanted nothing more than to go back right then. She hesitated before answering.

"I think I can stay until the end." David would take her home in a heartbeat if she asked, but he would also ask her a ton of questions on the way, questions she didn't readily feel like answering. Questions she was pretty sure she wouldn't have the answers to.

"You sure, baby?" David cooed.

Jewel nodded with a smile and reached for her fork. "Yes," she pushed it into the cordon bleu and lifted the bite to her lips. She couldn't taste the flavor as she chewed and swallowed.

In the home office on the first floor, Ella pulled out the drawers to the records. They kept files on the children. Not much, but enough paperwork to sometimes regret the decision to start the daycare. She wasn't sure what she was looking for. The fear in her gut told her that perhaps their center had more to do with Julianna's disappearance than she would like.

She stood in front of the record drawers for a while until she saw the old style large paper ledger for accounting. They made more than enough money to pay for a part-time accountant to keep their books, but Alan insisted that he'd do it. After two years of helping Ella to manage the daycare part time, he eventually turned to the center to help bring in better, full-time pay. He insisted that keeping their own records would help them save. She had never questioned him before, never had a reason to, until now.

Ella moved to the ledger and opened the book. She knew they had accounting software that Alan used, but he also liked to keep a hard copy of the money with the books. There was a stack of checks from the business check book. She saw slips of receipts. Under her breath, she read the memos to herself.

"30 Minutes, Jade," she frowned. Jade was a little white girl with auburn hair. She came three times a week part time, but never just for 30 minutes. Setting it aside, she flipped through more.

"Kristy," she whispered beneath her breath, staring at another receipt for cash payment. Those must have been made to Alan. She only ever took checks. She went through the rest of the receipts nestled at the front of the ledger book and pulled out every one written for cash. The others she recognized and had written herself. The ones for cash involved four little girls that came part-time, but none for the amount of time written on the memo. That didn't make sense to her.

"What are you doing?"

Ella jumped at the voice. The ledger tilted and crashed to the floor. The receipts floated, fluttering to the ground as if feathers. Ella snatched one from the air and shoved it out towards Alan. "What are these cash receipts for the part time girls?"

Alan's eyes widened. He snatched the receipt from her hand and bellowed, "Sit down!"

Ella jumped and stumbled back. Her feet caught the papers on the ground, and she slipped, falling into the computer chair.

Stooping down, Alan started to pick up the loose papers. He snatched at them, crumpling them into balls within his fists. He snapped his head towards Ella.

"Get out," he growled. Ella blinked at him, her breath coming in ragged sharp intakes of air. "Get out!" She jumped to obey and rushed out the room.

Once out, Alan stood and pointed towards her. "You wanted a daycare and that's what I gave you," his eyes traveled over his wife's short frame. "Go home." He slammed the door shut.

Ella stared at the closed door for several moments more with her body shaking before she could force her legs to move. She had seen her husband angry before but never did he yell at her. He could be controlling about the way he ran the family and the business, but she would have never thought he kept things from her. She remembered the puddle of urine on the basement floor and blanched.

11

Broken Love

The next thirty minutes were agonizing for Jewel. She forced smiles as the table conversed with each other, but she participated in none of it. While they ate their food, dread writhed in her gut.

"I think I might need to go home," Jewel whispered to David at length and regretted it the moment she saw concern and worry wash over his face. She had barely touched her plate. She knew she needed to eat, but her heart was too raw, her body too devoid of feeling to care. All she could remember was the darkness and intense fear from the girl in her vision. The feeling of being so alone, so lost and so confused, it was beyond paralyzing.

She avoided David's eyes looked around the table. She could feel him looking her over and felt the concern in the words he didn't say. He nodded meekly and then turned to face the table as she did.

"Looks like we're going to be heading out of here early," David began. There were a few murmurs of slight protest. Jewel saw Landra eyeing her curiously. She locked hair behind her ear and grabbed her clutch.

"Sorry, everyone. It was a pleasure to be here," Jewel managed. As she stood, David turned and placed an arm around her waist. As they moved through the banquet tables of the dining area, he moved his hand to the small of her back and massage lightly. He glanced at her several times, a look she initially tried to ignore. In the car, after she had pulled her seat belt across her body, David turned to her from the driver's seat.

"Are you going to tell me what's going on?"

Jewel frowned. "Please, David," she tried to meet his eyes but couldn't. Instead, she just held her head in her right hand. "Please, not right now. I have a splitting headache and I'm tired. I just want to go home."

"I care about you, Jewel," David's voice was unusually hard. "Can't you see that? I care about you and you're just pushing me away."

Jewel rubbed hard at her temples. "Honey, I just," she squeezed her eyes shut. The buzzing was starting to return. "Please, I have a terrible headache."

At her side, David fell into silence. He stared at her, breathing heavily before he turned and started the car. He drove in silence. As he pulled up to the outside of her apartment building, he idled the car.

"I can't keep doing this."

Jewel snapped her attention to David. He didn't look at her this time but stared out the front window of his SUV. Frowning, Jewel shook her head in confusion.

"You can't keep doing what?"

"This," he turned to her and pointed. "I love you, Jewel. You know that. I want a future with you and yet you refuse to let me in."

No, no, no. Not now. Jewel shook her head again. "Please. I just—I'm so tired."

"You're always tired, Jewel. You always just need time." Their eyes met, and this time, Jewel felt her resolve cracking. She saw the pain on his face, the agony. "I love you, Jewel," it was like a plea for her to come clean. But what exactly was she going to tell him?

"I don't understand what you're saying," Jewel said instead. She searched his face.

"If you can't let me in, then I don't see what I'm doing here. You don't want me—."

"No, David, that's not true," Jewel said quickly. Why didn't he understand that she was just going through some things? Why was he picking tonight? Why had he bothered her the night before? Every time he didn't get his answers, he was at it again. Didn't he understand he was just too much? Couldn't he back down, even just a little?

Turning from Jewel, David gripped the steering wheel. Did he expect her to leave after what he said? Confused, Jewel reached for his arm. In a rush, he pulled away from her and stared at her with wide eyes.

"I said I was done, Jewel," his voice was hard, yet somehow soft with remorse and anguish.

"What are you saying?"

"I can't keep doing this. I love you and you are pushing me away," his eyes pleaded with hers. "I'm done. We're done."

"No, no. Baby, you can't mean that."

"But I do, Jewel!" His voice was a shot of anger that ripped through the silence in the car. Jewel didn't understand how the night could have started so well, only to end like that. It didn't seem right. It wasn't fair.

"Please, just go," David whispered. He turned and took the car out of park. His jaw was clenched. Jewel thought about reaching for him again but reached for the door handle instead. She remembered how he recoiled from her touch, like she was a leper.

She lowered herself from the car and walked around the front of the vehicle. Her eyes stayed glued to David's face. He avoided making contact with her, looking away to the left, and then to the right. At the driver's side window, Jewel waited. He didn't turn to her. He didn't look at her, not even once. The vehicle pulled away and Jewel's heart shattered.

Her entire face was wet and tear-streaked by the time she made it to her room. She could barely even see where she was going. Her body trembled and rattled to the core. She found her pillow among her bed and vaguely remembered her phone. She slugged through the small clutch still in her hands, groping for her phone. She punched in Landra's number, her cries nearing hysteria.

"Jewel?"

She barely heard Landra answer the line. She tried to stop her tears, but couldn't.

"Calm down, sweetie. I'm still at the ceremony. I'll go to the bathroom so I can hear you better." In the next few seconds that followed, Jewel managed to stop gasping for air. The phone was pressed into her ear and her face was buried in the blankets and sheets of her bed. She hadn't even bothered to turn on her lights and could still feel her toes compressed in the heels she had chosen to wear for the evening.

She pushed the discomforting shoes from her feet and took a deep breath in the darkness of her bedroom. When Landra spoke to her, Jewel was finally able to hear.

"Is everything okay?" Landra asked immediately. Jewel could detect the faint hint of an echo where she was. Most likely a stall or in the bathroom by herself.

"No." Jewel sniffed. "It's not okay. I'm not okay."

"Well, talk to me. What's going on?"

"I had a vision in the bathroom. David dropped me off," Jewel began. She knew she was all over the place. This was just one of the things she wanted to talk about, but her mind could barely stay focused on a single topic. "He's mad at me. He said we're through," the cries and strain in her voice returned as she pushed out the rest.

Landra was silent for a moment. "David said he's done?" Her voice was more curious than Jewel would have liked.

"Yes. He said he's done with me. He's tired of me not telling him things. I don't know what to do," she heard herself as though she was an ant on the wall, listening in on the conversation rather than a part of it. Her voice was thin and strained, but even then, she couldn't mistake the undeniable whine it held. It disgusted her. She sounded so pathetic.

"Did you tell him you fainted in the bathroom?"

"No. You're missing the point—."

"No, sweetie," Landra interrupted, "I think *you're* missing the point. David is a good man and he cares about you," her friend's voice was soft, but the words seemed harsh.

Jewel pulled the phone from her ear and stared at it through the darkness. After a moment, she lifted it up again. "Are you serious, Landra? You're going to take his side?"

"Is this really about sides, Jewel?" Landra's voice was edged with a bit of annoyance.

Jewel shook her head. She couldn't believe it. The people she needed most were dipping out on her. "This is great," Jewel said thickly. "First David. Now you."

"No, Jewel. Please don't say that. You *know* I love you, Jewel. You know that," Landra's voice was rising on the other end. "And you and I both know that David is a good thing and you are pushing him away. You're sabotaging this thing, Jewel," Landra wasn't pleading anymore, but telling. "You're pushing him away so you can act surprised when he leaves, but he's telling you he wants to be with you and you aren't tell him the same back."

"That's not true," Jewel gasped. She told David all the time that she wanted to be with him.

"You and I both know you can't move forward unless you're ready to tell him what's going on."

"But I don't even know what it is, Landra," Jewel screamed suddenly into the phone. "I wish it would just stop!" She was crying again. She vaguely heard Landra speaking to her over the phone with a softer voice, but through her own tears and sobs, she couldn't make anything out. She pulled the phone from her ear and ended the phone call with a weak tap of her thumb.

She didn't know what they wanted her to do. They kept saying they loved her yet it felt as if none of them were truly willing to understand how she felt and what she was going through. David was so overbearing, always pushing for her to move forward with him. He wanted so much, but she had nothing to give. Didn't he understand that? Wouldn't he understand if he truly loved her?

Jewel pushed the phone from her body angrily. Her violent cries turned to silent sobs that racked her body. She wept until the tears dried and all that was left was the sound of her languid, pitiful moans. After time, those too subsided and she drifted into silence.

12

Heartache

Her heart was numb. Everything was cold. She had always feared what it felt like to lose a child. Now she knew. Sandy felt nothing. She was completely empty. She couldn't even help put her son to bed. She couldn't talk to him—not even listen to him. Everything he asked she didn't have the answers to. He asked so much. He wanted to know everything; but, they knew nothing. She knew nothing.

Her baby girl was gone. Her precious baby girl only six-years-old was gone—loose in the big world and it was likely that she'd never see her again. Sandy couldn't even fathom the thought. She remembered leaving Julianna at the daycare after she dropped Keith off at school. They had kissed, giggled, and then parted ways.

In the car, they had sung several songs together. Her daughter loved to sing. They joked that she was going to be a famous singer one day. She had an incredible, strong voice for a child.

At church, everyone commented on it.

Sandy couldn't believe that this was happening, that her little girl was really gone. From the hallway, William emerged. He glanced at his wife. She sat on the edge of the couch, hands in her laps. Her eyes were full, but he knew it was only because of fear. Her skin sagged and her face was blank.

He moved to her. No sooner than he sat down with her, she collapsed into his arms with tears falling and her body quaking. She was trying to say something. She was begging God, pleading with Him to keep her baby safe and that she would return.

William could only cradle his wife in his arms. He smoothed down her hair and cooed softly in her ear. He didn't quite believe in God the same that she did. Either way, if he were real, he hoped that his girl could be found. He couldn't even wrap his mind around the fact that a man might have stolen her, that a man might force his way on her...into her.

She was just a child. Things like that shouldn't even be possible. He pulled his wife into him and hugged tightly. Tears were streaming down his face now and he didn't even care.

He had put their son to bed. Keith was old enough to put himself to sleep, but under the circumstance, he wanted to let his son know that they were there for him. He asked questions about his sister.

Where was she? Was she at a friend's house? He had been tempted to lie, but no lie could sugar-coat the inevitable truth that had to come. So he did what his wife couldn't. He told his son the truth. His sister was taken from the daycare while they were at work and he was at school. Keith hadn't understood what that meant. Why couldn't they still go get her? *Because we don't know where she is, Keith. Someone is hiding her and they might hurt her.*

Keith didn't cry. William suspected it was because he just didn't get it yet. He still thought that she would come home, eventually. He didn't know what it could mean—and it could mean everything or nothing at all. The possibilities were endless. One thing was sure, however, when Keith could understand, he would be filled with anger and rage, just like William was now.

Sandy had always been the better one with kids. She had a mother's empathy in a way that William could never understand. He learned to trust his wife for what she knew about their children intuitively, and she seemed to believe that unless Julianna were returned, their family would be ripped apart. From Keith to Sandy and even to William. Not one of them would be spared from the terrible reality.

William didn't like that idea. He wanted to believe that it was just the fear talking. Fear could make you think crazy things. But somewhere, William felt she were alright. Their family wasn't complete without Julianna and if she was never found, he had no idea what would happen to them. He didn't want to go to that thought though. Not yet. His baby wasn't lost yet.

As William began to rock, holding his wife's limp body in his arms, he found himself hoping that his son would never get the chance to understand what happened. They were way too young for this. No family should ever have to feel what they felt or face the reality that was their world. As he clung to his wife, William found himself thinking about God. *Please, if you're out there...*

It wasn't pitch black anymore. The little girl that had come to her aid with water and food was no longer there. She wasn't sure when the girl left. She had cried herself to sleep after she had finished her food. When she awoke, the girl was gone and she was alone. In darkness. In silence.

The door to the empty room was ajar with a single stream of light cutting into the room. She was on a cot, something she would have gladly welcomed earlier if it weren't for *him*. He stood between her and the door. She couldn't meet his eyes. She couldn't even say anything, but she felt his eyes bearing into her body. She held her breath and tried her best not to breathe.

After a moment, she heard his feet shuffle. He moved away from her, towards the door. Now he was shutting it. She was even certain that he was locking it. She swallowed back a lump in her raw throat, something that took effort and hurt to do. She was alone again.

Jewel sat up with a start from her bed. It felt like she was drowning. She forced herself to breathe. It was like she was fighting for her life to get a breath. By the time she realized she had had another dream, and that she was still in her bed, lying in the dark, her face was wet with tears.

This was getting out of hand. Awake, asleep—she was getting no respite. The visions haunted her during the day and plagued her dreams when she tried to sleep at night. Through a foggy haze, Jewel sought for her phone in the covers on her bed. When she found it, she looked at the time. 2:16 am.

She groaned and closed her eyes. If this didn't stop soon, she was certain she'd have to seek outside help. She dropped herself into the bed, and then remembered how her night had ended with David. Were they really through? Or was he just angry?

Jewel touched her head as she thought about the two different possibilities. Her entire body seemed sore, with even her skin aching to the touch in certain places. She was certain it was just the stress of everything that was happening to her. She drew in a deep breath and tried to imagine a world where David wasn't in it. Nothing came to mind.

She loved him. She really did—did he not know that? She remembered when she first met him. Almost a year and a half ago. She hadn't even been looking for a relationship. A local venue was showcasing local singers and a band for their acoustic, piano, or a Capella night, and he had been there. He asked to share her table, and from there, an innocent conversation blossomed to creating time to come back and meet.

At first, she thought they were just becoming close friends. Whenever she was around him, in the beginning of their relationship, the other things in her life that had a tendency to bog her down didn't. She could enjoy life with him. That's when she knew he was special. He wasn't like the other men she had tried to date or tried to establish a relationship with. She knew that he really did love and care about her.

The tension came when he wanted her to commit to things, to him. Jewel wasn't a player. She was definitely the type of woman that only held eyes for one man, but to commit to something like that and open up completely? To pain, broken hopes and dreams? She didn't like that at all. She didn't think she was ready for that. And then, right about the same time, the visions and dreams started happening.

She didn't know who they were. She didn't understand why she felt everything the little girl did down to her fear, panic and terror. She felt it all and watched it all as if she were both on the outside looking in and then on the inside with the little girl.

Every time she saw her, she wanted to give her a firm hug. She wanted to draw the small child into her arms and never let go. In the dreams, she wasn't allowed to move. Just watch. Always watching, like it was some silent curse to see the pain this young girl was going through, and being so helpless to do anything about it.

That's probably what sickened her the most. The fact that she had to watch and couldn't stop anything. It wasn't right. She was certain the little girl was real. Whoever and wherever she was. If the visions meant she was in trouble, Jewel could only hope that it meant it was her job to save and help her.

Jewel sat up in her bed. That was something she had never quite thought of before. She knew the young girl was in a daycare. That's it. Was it possible to do something during her conscious that could help her? She had to try.

13

Grandpa Did What?

Driving the lone streets in the night, Ella glanced in the backseat. Her granddaughter sat quietly. After the police had been called, she was taken from the daycare and placed with the neighbors. She had picked her up to take her home after she left Alan at the daycare. Her daughter was divorced and in the service. Whenever she had to work overnight, or for unreasonable hours, her daughter came to stay with them.

Ella used to think it was a dream come true, getting to spend so much time with her precious granddaughter. Except as the young girl aged, her problems began to blossom. Her grandchild used to love visiting their house. Now Ella knew she hated it. That hurt her more than anything. The daycare was her chance to pour into children what she had missed from her own parents during her youth.

Her mother had been a nurse while her father was a union electrician. When jobs became scarce, he had to start traveling to distant cities for work. It put a strain on the family, emotionally and mentally; and then financially when her father had an affair and simply left her mother with three children.

Ella knew more than anything from growing up beside her mother how important good childcare was to single parents, especially mothers. That's why she loved the daycare so much. That missing little girl was not only a horrifying tragedy, but also a complete death of her dreams. Sill, Ella knew she would do anything to find her.

"Are you worried for that little girl?" Ella asked her granddaughter. Her voice split through the space in the vehicle like a ripple through time. The young blonde said nothing in return. She was quieter than normal. Ella forced a smile and bit back her frustration. She had never felt so hopeless in her life.

When they reached their home, roughly ten minutes from the daycare, Ella had fallen back into a stupor of silence. She wasn't sure if her granddaughter had had anything to eat, but at that moment, she really didn't care. She could have peanut butter and jelly for dinner. Ella's body was shaking internally. Once they made it inside, Ella motioned towards the kitchen.

"You can have P B and J for dinner, okay sweetie?" Ella sniffed and began to move to her bedroom, located across the living room. She dragged her foot across the tile of the hallway, and carpet of the living room. She could feel her granddaughter watching her. Was she thirsty too? "If you're thirsty, you can have cool-aid," she called. Anything to keep the girl away from her, from bothering her the rest of the night.

She was in the middle of the living room when she noticed her granddaughter hadn't spoken at all. Ella sighed. Maybe it was insensitive of her to be so emotionally drained. She turned and frowned with her brow pinching together. Her granddaughter's face was wet. She leaned against the wall with her back and cradled her torso in her arms. She was rocking back and forth.

"Samantha, are you okay?"

The young girl shook her head. Her eyes squeezed together tightly. Her rocking increased. The grip she had on her arms made Ella certain she would leave a mark. The girl's knuckles were white. The rocking bothered her. It wasn't the first time she had seen the girl rocking herself. Usually, she saw it at night when she checked on her before she went to sleep. She always thought it was because she missed her mother. There was something about it now that just seemed off.

"Samantha," Ella called, turning more completely to the young girl. "What's wrong?"

"I don't want him to hurt her like he does me," she said in a thin whisper. The end of her voice was swallowed in a loud gasp as Samantha gulped for air.

Immediately, Ella's body went tense. She took a step towards her granddaughter. Her body strained against the action. Everything about this just seemed...wrong. The tears of her grandchild's face, the rocking, her words. *I don't want* him...

"Don't want who, baby?" Even as Ella said the words, a chill clawed its way across her body. No. It couldn't be. She took another step towards Samantha, her mouth drying and her stomach turning. Everything inside of her wanted to ignore the situation, to pretend it wasn't happening; but, she saw more than just concern on her granddaughter's face. She saw fear. The missing girl was in trouble and Samantha knew where she was.

"You know where she is, don't you?" Ella said in a breath.

Like a dam breaking forth, Samantha cried and gulped back another breath amidst her tears. Her body was shaking violently. It was involuntary. Ella moved to her granddaughter's side and held her. Her mind raced with questions. How did she know? Was Alan hurting her? How long had it been happening? Why didn't she know? How could she *not* know?

Instead, all she could manage was, "I'm going to protect you. Help me help her. Tell me where she is." Ella cradled Samantha in her arms, but the girl's body was stiff and rigid. She was begging her grandmother not to tell Grandpa, asking her for forgiveness for being bad, for opening her mouth.

Ella shushed and cooed the young woman. She had no idea when Alan was returning. If he came home and saw them, she couldn't imagine it boding well for either of them.

Samantha's weight pulled against Ella as she tried to get the woman to walk towards her room. She didn't want her grandchild knowing that she was just as scared of her husband as she was of her granddad.

Samantha was beyond hysterical. Ella eventually stooped to scoop the child into her arms. She thought for a moment that the two of them should leave. They could run away. There had to be shelters they could escape to, a safe place for them to at least stay the night. No sooner than the thought came to her, she remembered Julianna.

Ella moved towards Samantha's room and ran a hand over the back of her head as she cooed to her and tried to bring stillness over her body. They couldn't leave. Not yet. They needed to find the little girl and then they would run away. She'd call her daughter in the morning. She didn't know where they'd go. Alan kept all the money. She didn't have her own accounts, just a debit card to their joint banking account that Alan handled exclusively. He said it gave him a piece of mind financially to handle all the money.

He had told Ella that he didn't want her to worry about anything. He wanted her to know that he was going to take care of her, no matter what; but, now it seemed everything he convinced her of when she didn't like how little freedom it gave her only served one purpose, and that was to keep her from being able to leave.

She received $50 a week for gas and it was usually just enough to drive to the daycare and back and twice to the store. Alan gave her $100 a week for groceries at home and $300 a week for the day care groceries. $300 was really pushing it, but he told her if they couldn't make a profit then they had no business to even have the center. That center was her dream so she pinched pennies and applied for subsidized help whenever she could to keep Alan happy with the daycare.

Holding her granddaughter tightly, Ella realized she was crying now too. All the pieces were adding up and she didn't like the reality. She didn't understand how she could have been so blinded by Alan's action. Controlling all the money while Samantha had suddenly stopped wanting to visit and spend the night with them.

Ella had been too focused on her dream to even see the signs. She just kept her husband happy. She wanted that day care so bad, and now an innocent girl's life was on the line.

"We have to save her," Ella said with a gasp. "We have to get her home to her mommy. When we do that, you and I will go away from here, okay?" Ella pulled away from Samantha and peered into the little girl's eyes. She was so brave for finally speaking up.

"I'm so proud of you," Ella said with a firm nod. "Did Grandpa say he would ever hurt you?"

Weakly, Samantha nodded. "I'm scared for her, Grandma," it was a whispered statement that chilled Ella to her core. She was afraid for *them*.

14
Who is this Man?

Alan came home much later than he should have, Ella noticed. In fact, there was no real reason for him to have sent her home first. On any other day, Ella would have kept her mouth shut and done what was necessary to appease him. Today, all the pieces were starting to fall into place. Everything made sense and she had no idea what to do.

She was lying in bed on her stomach when Alan entered. She kept her eyes shut and even squeezed them as light flooded the room. Ella didn't think Alan would check to see if she were awake, and she was right. The lights had been on for only a moment before they turned off. He dropped his body into the sheets. It didn't take time for her to realize that he had fallen readily asleep. How could he do that?

He took no shower, nothing. He just came in and went to bed. Like a child. It was like he wasn't even the slightest bit concerned about the daycare center being under investigation.

Even the word made Ella's skin crawl. Breathing was becoming laborious. She had to force air into her lungs, to help her chest expand with each breath.

It never crossed her mind before how she was always on edge around him. That was just the life she had come to adopt. Everything was necessary if she expected to keep her daycare. That was the carrot Alan always dangled in front of her. He criticized her ability to do anything other than take care of the children. That's how he gained control of the finances. He told her he was better at it.

He said giving the money to her like he did only ensured their success. He wanted to keep her from making mistakes, which is why he limited her access to funds. Yet every time she thought of leaving, the money was the first barrier she was never able to get over. And then there was her granddaughter, Samantha.

It was no secret that their marriage had been on the rocks for years. Ella hated every single moment of it, but he had promised her the daycare and he had delivered. She had always believed that that one single act must have meant he really cared. Was it all just for the children? To get closer to the children?

A sob threatened to escape her throat. A thick fog clouded her mind and hung heavily over her consciousness. Throughout the night, she didn't sleep. Not even once. Her body was tense with fear and apprehension.

She knew what she had to do and the thought only terrified her. She wanted to leave—to take her granddaughter and leave. She didn't know where any shelters were, but if she could just sneak away, the day care would close and they would be safe, right? No. There was still the little girl. Samantha told her where she was and Ella hated herself for not being more observant. How had Alan achieved so much control in her life that she was completely blinded by everything that happened? The very thought sickened her.

Periodically, Ella strained to catch the clock on the bed stand near Alan. Each time she managed a glance, only 20 or 30 minutes passed at a time. Being left alone with her thoughts, time seemed like it was dragging on. It was only 3:20 am. Ella took a deep breath and tried to roll onto her back. She pushed herself up with her palms and toes, trying her best not to disturb Alan.

It took her a full ten minutes to finally get situated into the position she wanted. She had been crafting a plan since the moment she laid down. Samantha told her that Alan had an extra key on his keychain. That wouldn't be hard to get. She knew better than to ever drive his car so he never guarded his things. He had his own room, his own things. She knew better than to mess with any of it. And like a prideful, arrogant man, he probably had everything out in the open.

His keys hung on the key rack right beside the door. The only thing she had to worry herself with was slipping out of bed without being detected. She was going to rush to the daycare and take the little girl home. Afterward, she was going to grab her granddaughter and leave. It was Thursday, so she didn't have much gas in the car, but she figured she could at least get to a police station in the next city over. Perhaps somewhere near Calumet or East Chicago. She didn't want anything tracing back to Alan. If he were found out, he'd make her life hell. Of that she was certain.

Lying on her back, it was a lot easier to check the time. She figured Alan must have come home around ten at night. She was normally the first one up to be at the daycare at six, but with the investigation and the missing girl, they had advised the other parents to find alternative arrangements until the next week when they would know more.

She thought for a moment that perhaps things might not be so bad after all. If she returned the little girl, her parents were likely to withdraw her from their care. They could still have the day care—wait. That wouldn't work either. Her grandchild wasn't safe, and neither were the other kids. If Alan captured a little girl, what would he do with someone else's daughter? Truly the man was out of control. Taking and hiding a child was simply beyond crazy; and, yet, what exactly had he been doing to Samantha? Her granddaughter hadn't been able to say. But, she didn't really need to say anything because Ella was pretty sure she already knew.

Her mind couldn't go there. She wouldn't allow it to or she might faint or pass out. It was too much—it was just too much. She didn't ask for this. All she wanted was a day care, to care for children in the way she knew her mother had wanted to care for her and her sisters when they were younger. Was that such a terrible thing?

She peered at the clock. 4:18 am. Now was as good of a time as any. Ella dropped a leg over the side of the bed. She did it slowly, sliding her leg across the sheets until there was no more bed beneath her leg. She started to move her other leg, the one closest to Alan.

He stirred, his head jerking. Ella held her breath and position. It was just a jerk. Her other leg was to edge of the bed. She dropped it over and used the weight to pull the rest of her body down. She slid off the side of the bed, her bottom landing first while her back remained flush with the edge of the bed frame. She waited, suddenly aware of her racing heart within her chest. It fluttered and rattled. She realized her entire body was shaking. She wasn't quite sure why. Was it adrenaline or was it fear? It didn't matter.

Alan hadn't shut the door all the way last night. He had left it cracked. That was good, at least for her. She could slip through, grab his keys and then rush out to the car from the backdoor through the kitchen. He wasn't likely to hear her leave.

Glancing behind her, Ella gulped and caught her breath. It was now or never. That little girl was counting on her. She pushed herself up and tiptoed towards the door. She didn't look back. She had to push it a bit to slip through, but it didn't crack or make any noise. Once out, she headed straight for the front door and grabbed all of the keys in one hand. She grabbed the second set of keys with her other and slipped them off the hook. Still silence.

She turned and headed towards the kitchen. She wouldn't stop. She just needed to get out. She drove a stick. She'd put it in neutral to get it to slide out the driveway and into the street. At least that was the plan. Their driveway wasn't that steep, but she hoped the weight of the vehicle would make it slid down the hill so she could start the car in the street and be gone. If Alan was still asleep when she returned—and she prayed that he would be—she could grab Samantha and leave.

She was already closing the back door when the thought came to her. She could get Samantha right now. Then, she wouldn't have to return. She could just escape. The kitchen door was already closed. It would at most be a 30 minute trip. Would Alan be up at 5 am, the time she was likely to return? She hoped not. She didn't want to go back inside and risk waking him up. That wouldn't bode well for anyone. First things first: she needed to free the little girl.

15

Free the Girl

Putting the car into neutral worked better than she thought it would. The car rolled out the driveway quietly and she used the steering wheel to back out and position the car on the street. Afterward, she started the car and broke the speed limit driving to the daycare.

At the time when they made the purchase on the house, it was in a fledgling neighborhood but hadn't always been. It was a great deal because there was so much that had to be done to it. Like a house bought for the sole purpose of upgrading and then selling it in better condition than it was purchased in for a significant return on investment. Except it was their daycare and there was no intention to resell. Alan made her do as much as she could by herself. That meant replacing fixtures, repainting, and gardening in the front and back. What she wasn't able to complete, to get help, she had to petition members of her church.

Alan made people think times were just hard and rough for them. They always seemed to live like there was never enough money. Yet her children were subsidized by state childcare checks to make it more affordable for working families and still Alan acted as if it wasn't enough. She began to wonder what he was really doing with all the money. And then there were those anonymous payments for cash. None of her parents paid with cash. What did that mean?

Ella turned off a main street onto a side neighborhood, the one housing the center. The horizon of the world was a bruised purple as the shades began to shift and lighten with the approaching dawn. She scanned the houses and vehicles of the street. The police cars keeping tabs on them last night was gone. She pulled into the driveway of the house and rushed around to the back.

Samantha told her there was a hidden room accessible through a utility closet in the basement. It was like a storm shelter. Ella remembered that room, a tiny crawl space too stuffy and small to fill a family decently. Still, it was nice to know it was there— yet she had completely forgotten about it.

Running through the house, Ella flipped frantically through Alan's set of keys. She wasn't sure which was which and tried them all at the door that lead to the basement from within the house. It had an odd placement, the last door in the hallway right before the stairs that led up to a master on the first floor.

It was a huge place, just the thing for a day care. Now Ella only hated it. After two different keys, one finally went in and turned. She felt like her heart was going to explode with the way it rapidly pulsed in her chest. She couldn't stop though. Once the door opened, she ran downstairs and looked around. It was just an empty room with a cot and a shelf full of cleaning supplies and old paint buckets.

Samantha said the extra room was down in the basement. Ella's memory of it was only foggy. She went to the shelf and tried pushing it. The cleaning supplies seemed heavier than they let on. She didn't have much time and thought about Samantha still sleeping at home. She cursed beneath her breath. She didn't understand why she didn't think to bring the child sooner. Probably because she had been so focused on returning Julianna to end the investigation. Alan would only make her life hell if any of this came to light and the day care were found out. She was certain she would never be able to get away then. She had to have a chance, and right now, it all depended upon whether or not the little girl was returned.

The shelf finally moved, but it heaved only a bit. Ella kept rocking it. She gripped the metal sides holding it up so hard that her hands hurt. Tears were streaming down her face, but she couldn't stop. Angrily, she pulled it towards her and it began to lean. She jumped out the way as it tipped over and crashed into the ground with a deafening sound throughout the quiet house.

There was the door. She found the keys on the ground with the tipped paint cans and leaking liquid soaps. Putting her ear to the heavy door, she listened. There was no sound. She hoped the little girl was still inside. She fumbled with the keys again and began to shove them into the door. The first three didn't work. The fourth did. She yanked the door open, her heart shattering as she saw the little girl with frizzled dark hair sitting in the middle of the floor in a puddle of what she could only assume was pee.

She didn't know what to say. The little girl only stared, wide-eyed. She didn't even move. Ella motioned her to her quickly.

"I'm gonna get you home," she choked out. She moved finally, the little girl. She started to stand but then froze. Ella nodded. "You're going to be okay. Just don't even tell anyone about this. Don't ever say where he hid you. Let's go. Follow me."

The little girl was on her feet now. Ella took her by the hand and led her up the stairs. She didn't bother locking the doors on her way out. As the screen door to the back door slammed closed, Ella froze. It had to be around 5:30 am now. She had no idea how much time she spent struggling with the metal rack in front of the door. Her time was running out. She needed to get the girl home and then get Samantha. She cursed herself for having not brought her grandchild. Her vision began to blur with tears as she rushed to the car with the little girl trailing behind.

"Do you know where you live?" Ella asked with a shaky voice. She didn't think to try and get the information before she left. It would have been in the child files of the daycare, which were probably in the room with the accounting paperwork. It just meant another set of keys and fumbling trying to get the door opened.

"Bear Creek Road," the little girl croaked.

Ella nodded. "And the number? Do you know your house number?"

The girl shook her head. "But I know my mommy's car," it was the most pitiful whimper—but it would have to do. Ella started the car and began to drive away. She had passed Bear Creek Road numerous times on the way to the grocery store at the nearest strip mall from the day care. It was about eight minutes away. She wondered if she could get there in five.

When she turned onto the road, she immediately cut her speed. The girl's father and mother couldn't know who dropped her off or where she came from.

"This is it. This is the road. Can you look out the window for your mommy's car?"

The girl nodded and sat up. Ella realized she hadn't even put her seat belt on, never mind the fact that she shouldn't have even been in the front seat—but all of that was entirely irrelevant. Nothing about this day should be happening. There shouldn't have been a little girl sitting in her own pee in a locked room in their day care's basement. But there was. Her husband shouldn't have ever...Ella shook her head. She couldn't go there. She just couldn't.

"Do you see the car?" Her own voice was struggling to remain together. The sky was shades lighter and it seemed like a race against the sun. "Is it a truck, SUV? What?" She was starting to panic.

"It's a van. Red," the girl was whining now too as if she felt the urge and plea in Ella's voice to find the house quickly. "There! There it is—Mommy!" The girl sat up quickly, on her knees. She was pointing at a van several houses away. About two or three. The lights were off and the block was silent.

"Okay. I need to circle around. I can't drop you off at the front." Ella pressed the gas to speed by the house. She circled around and stopped at the beginning of the block and then turned to the little girl as she let the car idle.

"Listen to me now, okay?" She cradled the girl's cheek in her hand. "I don't know what he did, but don't you tell anyone, do you understand? Don't tell anyone who dropped you off. Don't tell anyone where you were. Don't tell anyone you saw Samantha. Don't tell a soul. Okay?"

The small girl nodded, tears already falling rapidly from her eyes and down her swollen cheeks.

"You're so brave," Ella said quickly. She leaned across her and opened the door, nearly shoving the little girl out. "Run home and pound on the door until someone answers!"

The girl didn't need any more instruction. She took off, feet pounding the pavement towards the red van several houses away. The house was probably over 100 feet away and still, Ella could hear every pound the small girl's fist made against the door.

On the drive home, Ella's heart still raced while her body filled with dread. The sky was light blue. She didn't speed this time. More cars filled the roads as the rest of the world began their day. When she pulled onto her home street, she felt like she could fill nothing. She was completely numb.

She knew she had made a mistake. She should have taken Samantha with her. She couldn't keep herself from cursing the fact that she didn't. It didn't take her long to spot her house. The lights were still off. She parked the by the mailbox, just in case she could still get out, and left the doors unlocked.

Swallowing back a thick type of dread that had been building within her since the moment she left, she approached the front door. In her mind, she saw a vision of her closing the kitchen door. She should have just gone back inside. She was so worried about that little girl...

A tear escaped as she gripped the handle. It was still unlocked. For a moment, her heart perked up. Perhaps she was going to be able to still escape with her grandchild. The happiness lasted all for a second, just long enough for her to enter the house to see Samantha perched on the couch.

She didn't bother shutting the door behind her as she took a few steps in. Samantha was crying.

"What are you doing? Let's go!"

"Go where?"

Ella whirled around to the sound of her husband's voice. He had been waiting for her behind the door. The dread was back. She couldn't speak. She couldn't even scream.

"Where did you go?" He asked, approaching her.

Ella stumbled back and shook her head. Her throat was swollen shut.

"What did you do?" He growled, raising a hand. He swung it fiercely, connecting with Ella's cheek. She collapsed to the ground and only saw a blur before Alan was upon her. He grabbed at her neck, clawing and scratching her until his fingers found their way around and squeezed. She choked, coughed, and sputtered, her vision dimming.

In the blur of her eyesight, she noticed that her fingertips tingled and her head seemed to swell with blood, itching all over her pores. She heard a faint whimpering, a crying whine behind her. It was Samantha. She was begging her Grandpa to stop.

"I'll do anything," she pleaded. "Please stop!"

"Shut up, girl!" Alan squeezed harder. Ella's vision dimmed, and then blacked out altogether.

JALANA SHEREE WALSH

16

Knock at the Door

Sandy sat up with a start. Her body was shaking and her mind raced before she even knew what had awoken her. And then she heard it, frantic pounding. She turned to William and pushed.

"Get up. Someone's at the door."

William stirred and then sprang into action, nearly leaping out the bed before consciousness took over. He stared around the room, confused.

"What is that?"

"Someone at the door," Sandy repeated. She followed behind her husband. It didn't sound like an adult, but like tiny little fists beating away. She pushed past her William against his urging and ran to the door. She undid the locks and pulled the door opened.

"Mommy!"

The sound of her daughter's voice exploded into the silence. Sandy stared, and then she grabbed. She yanked her daughter into her arms and crouched in front of her. Pulling back momentarily, she looked into her eyes and then turned her daughter's head to the left and right. She didn't see any bruises.

She looked dirty though and smelled like stained urine. She pulled her daughter back into her arms and stood, crying freely now. She could barely hear the words she was speaking, but a laugh escaped her. William was at her side, touching and stroking, cooing and laughing and crying. Before they shut the door, Sandy scanned the road. She searched for anyone walking past in the early hours of the day, a loan car idling on the street, but there was nothing. The road was empty.

Inside the house, Sandy took a moment to look her daughter over again. William was at her side.

"Where were you?" He asked.

"Did someone drop you off?"

The little girl's body began to shake. She shook her head and said nothing. Sandy pulled her daughter into her chest again and cradled her head. Over her daughter's frizzy hair, she met her husband's eyes. They may have had their daughter returned, but they knew the nightmare was far from being over.

17
Breaking News

Jewel was up again at six. That was very early for her. She usually tossed and turned until she rolled out of bed after 7:30 needing to rush to work since it was nearly 30 minutes away. She decided that she would be early today and just rose the next time she started from her sleep.

It was more of the same dream, more of the same vision. She didn't know what it meant or how she could get it to stop. She trudged into the bathroom and absently brushed her teeth. She stood beneath the running water in her shower for longer than usual. Her body was sore from being tense. Her neck and shoulder muscles were tight. The water helped loosen them, but after minutes had drifted by, she finally turned off the faucet.

She remembered the conversation she had with David the night before. It wasn't the first time he had spoken about leaving. She didn't think it was a control thing. He was just getting desperate. He wanted to move forward and she didn't want to move anywhere. She liked things the way that they were. Uncertain. For some reason, that made sense to her. One day at a time.

Right now, there wasn't too much friction. Things weren't too deep. She couldn't really imagine herself married, having kids. The thought of having a child only gripped her with fear. She had counseled too many young women that had been used and abused. It comforted her soul greatly to be able to help those women find healing so that they could move forward and live a rewarding life, but for her, she felt a little stuck.

She treated her job like a penitence she had to pay, and she felt like she owed these women at least their healing. She took their recovery very seriously, perhaps even better than her own well-being. Landra always told her it wasn't good, but Jewel couldn't stop herself from doing anything but what she already knew.

Jewel dressed slowly, filling the time as she pushed through getting ready. It definitely helped that she wasn't running late. She'd have to stop and get a double shot espresso along with a coffee booster of some sort to help her get through the day. Last night was terrible.

Despite the considerable time advantage that Jewel had from waking up early, by the time she arrived at work, she barely arrived before her starting hour from the detours she made to get food and coffee. It was still early than normal and people were surprised to see her.

"We didn't know if you'd make it today," Kiara said. She was perched behind her normal position of the front counter. Mr. Pierce and Ronald were there too. Behind Kiara and attached to the top of the wall was a flat TV monitor which generally played soap operas and morning shows for waiting parents while their children received counseling.

Jewel noticed that everyone was watching it. Even Kiara's statement wasn't really an offer for a brief conversation, but more like an acknowledgment that she realized Jewel had arrived. Kiara was watching the TV and the four of them stood in silence watching the report.

As Jewel approached the desk, she glanced around for Landra. Her friend was nowhere to be found.

"What's this?" Jewel asked. She received a chorus of "shhh" from the other workers in the clinic. She glanced at the TV screen briefly and then continued to her office. She needed to speak with Landra.

Landra wasn't waiting for Jewel near her office like she had hoped. It wasn't like her friend to be late. She unlocked the door and set her things down before hurrying towards the front desk again. She spotted her friend this time, but she was equally taken with the news report. Jewel turned to the TV as she neared the front desk.

"What is it?"

"Will you please be quiet?" Mr. Pierce nearly snapped.

Jewel frowned, meeting Landra's eyes. She shrugged, and then turned to the TV. Jewel followed suit.

"The daycare, which has been in operation for the past 24 years, is facing serious investigations involving many of the children that were enrolled in its care. The owners of the business have been detained. Bail has yet to be set."

Pictures of the individuals were plastered to the screen. Jewel froze.

"Alan is 73 and has been charged with multiple accounts of

aggravated sexual assault and abuse with a rising count of at least 12 victims who were fondled, molested, and perhaps even digitally penetrated or more."

Jewel gasped, her hand flying to her heart. Mr. Pierce looked to Jewel.

"The courts have contacted the center to be the appointed counselors and expert opinion regarding the psychological state of the women and the children who are claiming the abuse."

She barely heard his words. The images of the daycare owners were taken away and replaced with the pretty brunette reporter with blood red lips. She began to recount information she more than likely had already repeated several times that morning.

Jewel felt Landra tap her side. She looked to her friend, still in shock.

"Everything okay?" Landra asked curiously.

Jewel's breath was caught in the back of her throat. *The visions are real.*

Landra chuckled. "You okay, Jewel?" Her voice pulled Jewel from her jumbled thoughts. She glanced at the TV. The report was over. Facing Landra again, she blinked back the gnawing grind in her stomach.

"I need to talk to you before we get started today," she began.

Landra nodded. "I was hoping you'd want to talk before your first appointment."

Jewel followed Landra into her office. Her head spun with the words of the TV report. Those faces seemed so familiar, and that daycare—she was certain it must have been the one from her dream.

"So how are you feeling today?" Landra asked as she moved to sit behind her desk. Jewel sat down across from her, running her fingers along her forehead.

"Not good. Sleep isn't getting any better," she spoke slowly. She couldn't get the TV report out of her head and her mind kept switching back to the picture of the owners.

"Have you talked to David?"

"David?" Jewel was confused at first, and then she remembered their big fight if she could even call it that. How could she have forgotten? She was just thinking about it earlier that day.

"Yes, the tall, dark and handsome man that wants you to be his main squeeze," Landra chuckled lightly before her face suddenly became serious. "You can't keep pushing him away, Jewel. One day he just won't come back."

Jewel nodded. She tried to follow her friend's train of thought, but the face of the daycare owners kept flashing in her mind.

"What do you know about that report?" Jewel asked.

Landra frowned. "The love of your life just told you last night that he was done and you're worried about a TV report?"

"Mr. Pierce said something about the courts contacting us for their trauma counseling?"

Landra shook her head harder this time. "Jewel, what is wrong with you?"

"What?" The question took her back. Landra was angry with her.

"Why do you do this to yourself? Work isn't going to keep you company at night!"

Jewel was silenced at the sudden rise in Landra's voice. Her friend had her complete attention.

"David loves you, Jewel. I know you know that. You have consistently chosen work over him time and time again. He has patiently waited for you and you have only hurt him," her voice softened. "You are purposefully sabotaging your happiness. Do you understand that? What would you tell one of the girls you counseled if they were in your shoes?"

Lowering her eyes, Jewel shifted uncomfortably in her seat. "I'd tell them that they were worth happiness," her voice cracked.

"Then why don't you believe it for yourself?"

Jewel touched her cheek and was surprised to find wetness there. She wasn't sure when she had started crying. It wasn't a hysterical cry like the night before, but whenever she blinked, more tears fell from her eyes.

"I have to pay for what I've done," Jewel managed.

Landra shook her head and stood. She moved around her desk and wrapped her arms around Jewel's frame.

"You need to forgive yourself," she whispered.

Jewel remembered the little girl from her dreams. If she could help out that poor, defenseless baby, she might just believe that she could be forgiven.

Landra's phone rang after silence had dropped upon them. She pulled away from Jewel and lifted the phone to her ear. For a moment, she was silent.

"Okay. I'll send her to your office right now," Landra's voice had returned to spotless professionalism. As she returned the phone to the receiver, she looked at Jewel and smiled.

"Mr. Pierce needs to see you in his office."

Jewel drew in a deep breath and nodded. "Promise me you'll call David today." Jewel frowned and opened her mouth. "Promise me!"

Laughing, Jewel nodded and stood. "Alright. Alright. I promise. I'll call David and try to work this out."

18

The Investigation Begins

"You needed to see me, Mr. Pierce?" Jewel asked after rapping on her boss's open door. He looked at her momentarily and then smiled broadly. "Yes. Please come in and have a seat."

Jewel moved into the office and sat down in a chair. Behind his desk, Mr. Pierce had several manila folders open on the desk with loosely printed papers strewn about.

"This morning is going to be a busy one for me," he chuckled at length. "Just give me a moment," he muttered. He organized the folders and papers loosely before he turned to Jewel completely. "This day care case is huge, Jewel. Investigators want preliminary screenings on all children involved by noon. They're really trying to move forward with some tangible charges on these owners as soon as possible."

Nodding, Jewel leaned forward. "I'm ready to do whatever is necessary."

"That's good. You're the best therapist we have for cases like this. Her name is Lexy. She's the great-granddaughter of the daycare owner. It's her case that is leading the investigation. Her mother says he touched and raped many girls there."

Jewel's face twisted and frowned. She felt her stomach lurch. Mr. Pierce nodded.

"I know. It's utterly disgusting. Do you think you can get the mother and daughter started with an intake interview so we can have something to give the police? They want to make an official press release sometime this afternoon. The city is outraged."

Jewel nodded. "I can only imagine. This is a daycare," she fell into silence. After a moment, she asked, "How soon will they arrive?"

"They're already on their way. Give them ten or so minutes."

Her head began to spin. "Goodness. Okay. I need to get going then. I'll have to verbally ask the questions, maybe record it and go back over it as I fill out their paperwork. Am I'm just interviewing the little girl?"

He shook his head. "The mother too." Jewel was about to leave the chair, but at Mr. Pierce's words, she stopped.

"Why?"

"Police think she's somehow involved too."

To keep herself from saying more, Jewel pressed her lips together and only nodded. This was the part of her job she always hated. Many people went their whole life without ever being subjected to the harsh realities she saw day in and day out. It was beyond disgusting but if it weren't for people like her willing to stand in and help the victims find recovery, the cycle of abuse would only continue.

In her office, Jewel rummaged through her intake paperwork. She grabbed assessments for children and adults. She didn't generally work with adults—their feelings were way too complicated and hardened for her to handle—much like herself. She mused at the thought. Once she had the forms and paperwork she needed, she began to organize them on her desk. It was then that she saw the clients.

She noticed the mother first, a blond with tired, dirty blue eyes. She was beyond worn and her entire demeanor hinted at a deep sadness and pain. The sight accosted Jewel. Her office door was already open. She was certain Kiara would have ushered the mother and daughter to her office, so she motioned for them.

"Good morning. I'm Jewel," no sooner than she had said it, she immediately regretted her choice of words. The mother grimaced.

"It ain't a good morning, Ma'am," she spat. She roughly nudged her daughter to take a seat while she took the other.

Jewel nodded. Her smile dropped. The woman was right. There weren't pleasantries in all of this.

"Forgive me for that," Jewel tried to start again. "Let's get right to business. Who wants to go first?"

Her mother jerked her head towards her daughter. "Tell her what you told me, Lexy-lou."

Jewel smiled. Although the mother was rough, she could still hear the love of her daughter in her voice. Turning to the girl, Jewel took her in. She looked mixed and had tight, curly hair and tanned skin.

"You're beautiful," Jewel commented. The little girl squirmed at the words. She didn't believe it.

"Pop-pop touches me," she said plainly.

Jewel nodded. "Do you want to talk to me about it?"

The little girl shifted in her seat. She looked to her mother, but the lanky woman didn't say or do anything. At length, the little girl turned back to Jewel. Her eyes misted over and she gave a firm nod.

19

Revelation of Secrets

"Would you like something to eat or drink?" Jewel asked the young girl. She shook her head. Taking a deep breath, Jewel arched her back. "Okay, you're so brave for doing this," she commented. The little girl only blinked. "I'll let you begin. You can tell me whatever you like." Jewel positioned a sheet of paper in front of her and grabbed her pen. As a second thought, she reached into her desk for a small digital recorder. She pressed record and laid the machine down in the middle of her desk.

With a sniff, the little girl shrugged her shoulders. "Pop-pop touches me," she repeated. "I don't like it."

"Can you tell me where he touches you? You can just point."

The girl pointed at her chest. After a moment of hesitation, she moved her hand down, towards her lap. She glanced towards her mother and swallowed back.

"He touches you along your chest?" Jewel asked.

The girl nodded, and then said, "Yes. And he touches me down here too."

Jewel nodded, breathing deeply. She didn't understand how anyone could justify abusing the innocent, but she knew all too well from the countless women she counseled that it happened every single day. The only atrocity greater than that were individuals who knew or suspected and never did anything to stop it.

"I don't like it," Lexy said softly. "I don't like it when he touches me."

"I asked him not to," the mother spoke up before Jewel could address Lexy's statement. Her tone was hard and remorseful. Facing Lexy's mother, Jewel waited for more, but the woman said nothing else.

"You mean you asked him not to touch your daughter?" Jewel asked. The woman nodded. "Did you have reason to suspect that he would?"

The woman froze at the question. She reluctantly nodded. "We've been staying with my grandparents since Lexy was born. Her father was a deadbeat and I needed a place to stay until I got on my feet. I didn't trust my granddaddy but," she shrugged, "I needed a place to stay. I begged him not to touch her. I begged him," her voice snapped at the last word.

Jewel nodded and glanced to Lexy. The little girl sat rigidly in the chair with her mother behind her.

"There were many," her mother said, touching Lexy's shoulder. "There were so many more. I just couldn't take it. He promised me that he wouldn't. He promised, but he lied because he did," she cringed as she spoke and tears hovered just behind the surface of her eyes.

Jewel tried asking Lexy more pointed questions, but with her mother there, the little girl wouldn't offer more than what she did. She made note that they would need to interview them separately. What she had received so far was more than enough to help the police get their charges together.

"Thank you for coming in," Jewel said as she stood. She looked over the mother carefully. "I'm sure I'll be seeing you again as we move forward in the investigation. What I have here is enough."

The mother nodded. "C'mon, Lexy-lou," she motioned to her daughter to join her side as she moved towards Jewel's office door. She paused and faced Jewel again. "Maybe this will finally stop him from hurting more."

Jewel nodded quickly. "Yes. This is why we're here," she looked deeply into the mother's eyes, and then realized she had never gotten her name. "I'm sorry, what did you say your name was again?"

As the woman opened her mouth to speak, Jewel's phone rang. She missed the woman's answer over the obnoxious ringtone. It seemed louder than usual. Jewel lifted the phone to her ear. As she did, the woman and her daughter slinked out the office.

"New Hope Counseling Center, Jewel speaking. How may I help you?"

"It's David. Do you have a moment?"

Jewel's breath caught in her throat. She didn't think she would be expecting a call from him anytime soon. "Yes, of course," Jewel stopped the recorder on her desk and looked out her door. Lexy and her mother were long gone. Near the end of the hallway, she saw Mr. Pierce standing by the front desk. She knew he'd expect a briefing as soon as she got off her phone call.

Turning into the phone, Jewel whispered, "We were just handed a big case with the city. I don't have much time, but you can tell me what you called for. Please?"

David was silent for a moment. "I wanted to apologize for my behavior last night," he said softly. Even as he spoke, Jewel felt her heart melting. "I love you, Jewel. I just wish you knew how much. Can you call me later when you have more time to talk?"

She nodded, forgetting that David wouldn't be able to see her through the phone. "Of course. I'll talk to you later," she said softly.

"Thank you, Jewel. I love you," David said. He waited as if hoping for more from Jewel. She didn't say anything, she simply smiled and lowered the phone back to the receiver. She took a deep breath and stood. She grabbed the digital recorder and headed out her office towards Mr. Pierce.

"The police department just released the official charges through a press release," Landra said before biting into a cordon blue deli sandwich.

Jewel's eyes widened. "I didn't hear. How many counts?"

Solemnly, Landra shook her head. "You don't want to know," she lowered the sandwich and reached for her drink.

With a sigh, Jewel lifted a French fry from her plate. "That many?" Landra nodded with disgust. "I can't believe a grandfather would do this to his great-granddaughter."

"Didn't you say that her mother said there were more?"

Jewel chewed on the edge of the French fry absently. She nodded at length. "She said there were many, many more."

"Why do you think she stayed if she suspected it?" Landra took another drink, a flavored cola.

"I get the feeling that she was likely a victim herself at some point."

Landra frowned. "That is so sad." Silence fell between them. She thought about the dreams that she had been having.

"I've been keeping something from you," Jewel said softly. She had Landra's full attention.

"Is it about you and David? Are you getting married?" Her friend's voice ran together excitedly.

Jewel chuckled. "Oh heavens, no. I can't even think of that right now." Landra's face fell. Taking a deep breath, Jewel straightened her back and faced her friend. "I've been having very disturbing dreams," she hesitated, and then added, "and visions too."

Landra's brows furrowed. She crossed her arms and nodded for Jewel to continue.

"Last night, at the dinner, I had one in the bathroom."

Landra's eyes widened. "Is that why you passed out?"

"I think so," Jewel commented softly. "Sometimes I get really dizzy before I see one too—a vision, I mean." Jewel looked down. She had always wondered how the conversation would go when she finally talked to Landra about it. As far as she could tell, it was going pretty well. "Sometimes I get confused when they come. They take a lot out of me."

As she finished talking, silence rejoined them. They were in a downtown coffee shop enjoying the lunch hour. The place was scarcely populated with other working individuals from the same downtown region of the city, but, for the most part, voices were low, and café sounds were light. It was just another weekday afternoon.

Finally, Landra spoke, "What are the visions of?" She met Jewel's eyes. There was a concern, and yet a deep interest.

Taking another deep breath, Jewel moved onto another French fry. She didn't think she was really that hungry, but she knew she had to eat something or she would feel the hunger ten times worse later on.

"Well, they're of a little girl." Even talking about it seized her heart. Jewel rubbed a hand into her chest and forced herself to continue. "It's the same little girl in every dream. Whenever it plays, it starts at the same point, walking down a hallway and some stairs where," she paused, "where she sees something bad. Horrible." Landra listened silently. She encouraged Jewel to continue. "I think she walks in on a young girl getting raped."

Landra gasped. "Oh my goodness," she breathed and said nothing more.

Jewel fidgeted, feeling the same familiar feelings from the little girl in the dream start to creep over her. Suddenly, she didn't really want to finish. She looked into Landra's eyes. Her friend nodded gently.

"I'm listening," Landra said quietly.

Jewel blinked back tears that threatened to rise to the surface. She had never voiced the dream out loud before.

"It's just that I've had this same dream for years, Landra," Jewel sighed. "For years. Sometimes there are periods where I sleep fine, other times, usually when I'm romantically involved, it comes back every night. This is the worst it's ever been."

Landra nodded. "Is this why you can't sleep at night?"

Jewel nodded. "I think so," Jewel had long ago abandoned the French fry. She twisted a napkin in between her fingers instead. "My mother always used to tell me that God will sometimes speak to us through dreams," her voice was feather-lite as she spoke of her mother. "I used to hate the dream—still do, but now I wonder," she paused, "do you think that it was maybe preparing me for Lexy? I wish you could have seen the little girl, Landra."

With a shrug, Landra reached for her drink. "I don't know, Jewel. Have you ever told David?"

With a quick shake of her head, Jewel looked away. "I've never told anyone. Just you."

"Maybe you should tell him."

Chortling, Jewel breathed a sigh and nodded. "I know I should." She remembered his phone call. "He called me today."

Landra perked up. "Oh?"

"Yes. He apologized for last night."

"Really?" Landra chuckled. "You completely check out on *him* and he comes back and apologizes," she laughed. "He totally loves you, girl."

Jewel giggled and agreed. "I know. I should try and plan a do-over tonight with him or something."

Landra nodded in agreement. "Absolutely. Take him to another nice restaurant or something."

"Okay. It's a date," she chortled again. "I guess I should call him and see if he'll be my date—."

"You know he will be," Landra said matter-of-factly.

Jewel smiled. It was times like these that she realized the wonderful blessing she had in Landra's friendship. "Any ideas for a restaurant?" Jewel lifted her sandwich and opted for a bite.

Landra nodded eagerly. "Eddie Merlot's. It's in Englewood Illinois. Not too far. Lots of great wine and meat."

Jewel laughed. While other women they knew were hyped on the latest diet fads and raw food diets, Landra was still a meat girl down at heart.

"You're my favorite friend," Jewel smiled. Landra giggled in response and continued to eat.

After lunch, the women headed back to the counseling center. Jewel had more group counseling and a formal report to write for the police investigation. Before she began to settle back into her work, she lifted the phone and dialed David's number. He answered readily.

"David speaking," his voice was a forced calm. Jewel knew he would know it was her calling.

"Hey, babe," she said with a soft giggle. "I didn't want you to think I had forgotten about you." She heard a sigh. "Do you want to try last night again? Landra mentioned there's an excellent restaurant in Englewood."

"That's 30 minutes away, isn't it?"

"Yes," Jewel played with the phone cord, "but I like driving with you," she added sweetly. She could practically feel David's smile on the other end of the call.

"I'd love to then. If you tell me the place I can make the reservations."

"That's sweet, baby; but, I'll take care of this one," Jewel smiled. She really did love David. "I have to get going though. I have a lot of work to catch up on."

They ended the call shortly afterward and Jewel began to work. She paused about half an hour into her report of her interview with Lexy and her mother and made reservations online for the restaurant. She loved feeling like she accomplished something great. By the end of the day, her report had been finished and she had completed yet another successful group therapy session. It was times like these that made her feel like her life was worth something and that she was doing something good.

Every time she helped another young woman receive healing, she really felt like she was paying it forward. She was giving these women a chance at a new life they deserved. She knew better than anyone that a lack of healing could keep someone from their true potential. If it weren't for the work that she did, the girls she counseled would likely end up in abusive, dead-end relationships. She wanted them to have a chance at life itself, a chance at true happiness.

Later that evening, Jewel met David for dinner at Eddie Merlot's in Englewood. It was a great restaurant with just the right type of atmosphere which helped Jewel reconnect with David. They sat beside each other, holding hands while they waited for their food to arrive. Jewel had her head on David's chest. She loved sitting next to him. His body was the perfect image of strength in her life.

He took a drink of his wine and sat his glass down. As he did, he looked down at Jewel and smiled.

"I'm glad you're in a better mood," he whispered, his voice low.

Jewel searched his face and then placed a hand on his chest. "I'm sorry for making you feel like I don't want a future with you," her voice was a thin whisper. "I wish you knew how much I care for you, David."

He touched her hand and massaged it gently. His touch was electrifying. "Why won't you just let me in?"

Jewel looked away and pressed her head into his chest. "It's just not that easy sometimes," she said with a breath. She thought about her visions and about Lexy. She wanted to tell him, but couldn't. Landra was different. They had been friends for years. She knew there was nothing she could ever do that Landra wouldn't judge her for. Reprimand, maybe, but never judge or condescend.

She had been through many relationships before and for one reason or another, they never worked out. They had been with good men too. Men with promising futures and weren't a bed of excuses and dreams without action. She felt that as soon as they discovered the real Jewel, she lost their interest. They lost interest in *her*.

The dream was something Jewel had never mentioned to anyone before until earlier that day. How could she really expect anyone else other than her best friend to know and understand that?

David reached for Jewel's face and stroked the bottom of her chin. He tilted her chin up and their eyes met. Leaning in for a kiss, he pushed his lips against hers and breathed her in. "I love you, Jewel. But I can only get as close as you let me."

His words ran like a shiver down her spine. Her body quaked slightly as he pulled away, his eyes still locked on hers. That look was one she had seen so many times before. But there was something different about it this time. It was *deeper* somehow. He meant every word of it.

20

It's a Small World Daycare

The next several days at work passed without many incidences. Her dream had ended its cycle. This was the time she looked forward to most. Jewel never knew what happened to the little girl after she returned home. The dream only ever took her through the beginning and then the end. After that, it was nothing but silence, nights full of deep sleep and restful nights.

She was also never really sure what prompted the dream sequence to begin again. If she could have avoided that part, she would have. Instead, she just learned to deal with the dream sequence as it came. In her office, Jewel sat her pen down. She had just finished an entry in her journal:

The dream sequence finally ended. For the last three nights, I've slept better than I have in a long while. David and I seem to be doing better and I just recommended that one of my clients stop full treatment here.

Jewel looked back over the entry. It wasn't the first time she had written similar words down. She lifted the pen again and continued to write:

I wish I could believe that this was the end of it, but I know that it would only be wishful thinking. The dream will start again, and when it does, it'll claim my sleep, my emotions, and my mind. I feel like I'm going crazy sometimes...

Her phone rang. Immediately, she reached for the receiver and pressed it into her ear.

"New Hope Counseling Center, Jewel speaking, how may I help you?" The standard greeting rolled off her tongue easily.

"I'm Detective Banes, assigned to the It's a Small World Daycare Case."

Jewel nodded into the phone. "Yes. Is this about Lexy?" There was a brief period of silence on the other line. Jewel decided to continue, "I've met with her twice now without her mother. I've been able to extract more statements, but it's still difficult because she's really young and confused."

"Actually, Ms. Kennedy. I was calling to see if you could come to the station so that we could speak in person."

After a quick glance at her clock, Jewel took a deep breath. "Um, alright, I guess. This is about the daycare case?"

"Yes, ma'am. You'll receive more information when you arrive."

Jewel glanced at the clock again. It was an hour before lunch time and her next client wasn't due to arrive until two in the afternoon. "I need to check with my supervisor, but I should be cleared to take a trip to the station. Can I have your number?"

The officer relayed his number and then disconnected the call. As she suspected, Mr. Pierce gave her the time needed to visit the station. Thirty minutes later, she was walking into the front doors. She had called Detective Banes on the way to make sure he was there to greet her. As she walked into the building, a tall, stalky man came to meet her at the door.

He had a firm, warm handshake and dark, spiked hair. His blue eyes welcomed her with a friendly gaze. Jewel couldn't help but return his smile.

"Can you follow me, Ms. Kennedy?" The man turned and led Jewel through the main waiting area and through a small door. He quickly turned to the left and entered a room where another officer sat waiting. There were two manila folders on the table. Detective Banes turned and motioned for Jewel to take a seat at the table side closest to the door while he joined the other officer across the table.

Jewel approached the table curiously and then sat down. "How can I help you guys? You said this wasn't about my newest client, Lexy, or her mother," she wiped at her nose, "I'm just not sure how much help I can be for you."

"Straight to the point," Detective Banes nodded positively towards the other officer. "This is my partner, Detective Jones," he nodded towards the man at his left. He was a little heavier set with darker, greasy hair and glasses. Jewel offered her best smile and shifted in her seat before giving Detective Banes her full attention again.

"Ms. Kennedy, we've seized the records of the daycare for the past 25 years," the Detective said with authority. "We've asked for you to come in because we're reaching out to previous attendees."

Jewel blinked. The Detective finished his line and then waited, but Jewel didn't understand what he wanted. She chuckled nervously. "I've never attended It's A Small World Daycare," she said finally.

The two officers looked at each other dubiously. Detective Banes motioned towards the folders. "Our records indicate that you attended the daycare for three months around the time that you were six years old."

Shaking her head, Jewel stammered. She felt a buzzing begin faintly near the back of her head. She tried to shake it away. "I don't ever remember going there. Um," she sighed exasperatedly. "I know my parents used to live near there," she paused, "before my mother died of cancer. My father has since moved now. We never went there," she shook her head again. "No, my brother and I never went there."

The Detective's face never changed. He opened the manila folder with ease and lifted the first page. Jewel saw that it was a black and white photocopy page of an old news report. He turned it to Jewel and slid it in her direction. She skimmed the headlines: MISSING: LITTLE GIRL FROM LOCAL DAYCARE.

The picture, although heavily blotted in black ink, was of a little child: a little girl with fuzzy pigtails, bright eyes and a beautiful smile.

The buzzing was starting to grow. Jewel looked at the Detective, and then to the paper. She felt like it couldn't have been real, but that was her picture.

"I don't understand," she said after a moment. "How is this possible? I never went missing as a child," she shook her head. "I would remember this."

The cops exchanged another look. Detective Banes addressed Jewel again. "Ma'am, according to this newspaper clip, and the testimony of the daycare owner's wife herself, a little girl was reported missing October 8th 22 years ago."

Jewel shook her head again. The men's faces were no longer clear and she felt a heaviness looming in front of her head. Jewel stood abruptly, knocking her chair down. She didn't bother to excuse herself.

"I need to make a phone call," she muttered. Her words ran together. She heard two more sets of chairs push against the tile floor, and then Detective Banes's voice calling after her seconds later.

"Ma'am, are you going to be okay?"

Jewel stumbled to the door and grabbed at the handle.

"Phone call," was all she could manage. Outside the door, her legs gave way beneath her. She fell and her legs crumpled beneath her body. She managed to break her fall with her palms. Her breathing slowed. The door behind her opened. Faintly, she heard a deep, grating voice. Heat rushed over her and her body swayed.

There were more sounds, directions, and orders, but near her, Jewel only felt a dull silence. She stayed in the position until the waves of heat stopped washing over her frame. Slowly, the sound came back to her. Someone stopped in front of Jewel and sat down a short, plastic cup of water. She didn't know if it was a man or woman. She only saw the pointed tips of their black shoes.

Jewel kept her face to the ground and focused on taking breaths. She knew she had come close to passing out. Everything was coming back into focus. She heard Detective Banes behind her. He was requesting information for a state certified therapist. Jewel wrinkled her nose and felt a surge of anger wash over her; yet, her mouth was too dry to say anything. At length, she reached for the clear cup with a shaking hand and managed to drink the water. Her throat was sore suddenly like it was sliced raw. She continued to drink until the cup was empty.

Behind her, she heard Detective Banes speak. "Are you okay, Ms. Kennedy?"

"Yes," she said with a gasp. Jewel glanced around her. Whatever commotion that had come while she had almost passed out had gone. There was no one else in the hallway except the two officers behind her.

"I need to make a phone call," Jewel squeaked.

"We'll be right inside, Ms. Kennedy," one of them said in response. It didn't sound like Detective Banes' voice. She heard the door behind her shut. Slowly, Jewel forced herself to stand. Her head was still a bit lightheaded, but she ignored it and reached for her phone within the purse she had draped across her body.

Her fingers moved through her phone menus and selected an old number she hadn't dialed in a long time. Once the phone was ringing, she raised the device to her ear and sighed heavily. After three rings, the line opened.

"Jewel?" It was an old, weathered voice that greeted her.

"Hey, Dad," Jewel said softly.

"Sweetie," her father gasped a response. She heard the happiness in his tone. "It's been so long since I've heard your voice. How are you?"

Jewel felt herself overcome with a rush of emotion. Her eyes welled with tears. Closing them, one escaped and slid down her cheek. Jewel swiped at it.

"I miss you, Daddy," her voice cracked.

"Oh, sweetie." her father's voice cooed. "Why don't you call me more?"

Jewel's shoulders heaved. Every time she thought her life was finally getting back on track, something happened that knocked her off course. It hadn't even been a week since her last dream and already, she knew they would begin again.

"I don't know what's wrong with me, Daddy," Jewel whimpered.

"Oh, baby," her father took a deep breath of air. "Your miss your mother, don't you? I miss her too, sweetie."

Jewel remembered that the date of her death hadn't passed too long ago. She opened her eyes and forced a resolve to come over her. "This isn't about Momma, Daddy," Jewel remembered the news that Detective Banes gave her. "I'm at the police station right now."

"Oh no. What happened? Is this your one phone call?" Her father's voice changed suddenly to grave concern. "Baby, what's going on?"

Jewel chuckled. "I'm not in custody, Daddy. I just," she took a deep breath and remembered the daycare, "Have you heard about It's A Small World Daycare Center?" She was met with abrupt silence. She couldn't even hear her father breathing anymore. "Daddy? Are you there?" She heard a small exhale, but there was still silence. "Are you there?" She asked again.

"I'm here, Jewel. It's all over the news, sweetie. It's bad," her father finally answered.

Jewel nodded. "A detective called me in for questioning," there was more silence, but Jewel continued talking. "He said I used to go there, to that daycare. He showed me a flyer and everything," Jewel's voice began to run together. "I told him I've never been there...right? I've never been there, right, Daddy?" Jewel gripped at her shirt, twisting the fabric around in her fingers. She waited eagerly for her father to reply, but he didn't. Instead, she just heard slow, steady breathing.

With a deep intake of air, she heard her father begin to speak, "You used to go there, Jewel."

Jewel shook her head. She wasn't going to believe it. She would have remembered if that were the case. "No. Why don't I remember? They said I went missing October 8th 22 years ago. I don't remember anything. They told me I was six—I would have remembered. I don't remember anything," she repeated. Anger and fire were in her voice.

"Calm down, baby," her father said softly. Even his gentle command fed the anger in her veins like gasoline on a fledgling fire. Jewel clamped her jaw shut and clenched her teeth. "You used to go there," he repeated. "You went missing during the day. Around lunch time they said, goodness. It was so long ago," her father shuffled on the other line. "You were missing for almost 24 hours."

"24 hours?" Jewel's voice was a ghastly whisper. "How?"

"I don't know how, baby. The cops searched the daycare—the house. They found nothing. It was the worst time ever. It almost killed us, sweetie. I didn't think we were going to make it through. Your mom," he paused and swallowed back, "your mom was going out of her mind. She cried for hours. Keith was neglected and ignored—it was such a terrible time. When you returned, we were just so happy to have you back, that we," he paused again, his voice beginning to crack, "we questioned you, authorities questioned you, but you provided no answers."

"Weeks went by, Jewel," her father continued, "months and years and you never said a word about that place. You never told us what happened. We wondered, authorities wondered," he offered her a soft sigh, "we both decided that we would never talk about it unless you talked about it first. But you never did. At least until now."

Jewel couldn't stop shaking her head as she listened to her father's calming voice. He was so gentle with her, but even then, anger was in her bones. Yet, it was slowly being replaced by another emotion she had only felt from within her dreams: paralyzing fear.

"So you have no idea what happened when I was gone?" Jewel asked the question although she wasn't really sure she believed she was even missing. She never remembered being away from her father and mother, not even once. She didn't do sleepovers in middle and high school. She tried, but she never followed through. Seeing her parents getting ready to drive away had always frightened her so girls always came to her house.

"No, sweetie. I'm afraid I don't know what happened. You never told us." Her father paused before continuing, "What have the officers told you?"

"Nothing, just that I was there and they want to ask me questions about the place."

"Hmmm," her father mused on the other line. "You should work with them, baby. This might be good for you."

Jewel frowned at her father's words, but somewhere in her heart, she worried that he might be right. "How's Keith?" Jewel asked, changing the subject.

"He and his wife are great. Their baby girl just turned two. When will you come over? And bring that man, David so we can see him?" Her father forced a calm voice, but she knew that he worried he was treading the line. Jewel never discussed her personal life with them. She just didn't. It seemed that the moment she found a shred of happiness, it was gone and she didn't want to lose David. She never intended for him to see her family. To think of letting him in so close knowing that he would just disappear as the rest had—it was just too much to bear.

"I don't know, Dad. Do you have any pictures of her? What was her name again?"

"Marissa. You know, we miss you, sweetie. Why have you cut us off?"

Jewel blinked back new tears that threatened to return. "I'm just going through some things. My life isn't," she shook her head. Her family wouldn't understand. "I just need some time, Daddy. Can you tell Keith that? You guys know I love you. But things right now," Jewel sighed, "I love you guys so much."

"Why don't you just come over this weekend? Do you have work? We can grill out. Play some games," he made a sound that Jewel was certain was a mixture between a chuckle and a cry.

She couldn't keep the tears from falling. She didn't remember the last time she had seen her father and brother. He wasn't even trying to hide the strain in his voice. He was begging her, pleading with her to let him see his daughter again.

"Daddy, you know I can't."

"No, I don't, Jewel. Baby, please—."

"Daddy, I have to go," Jewel pulled the phone from her ear and quickly ended the call before a cry escaped her throat. She crouched to the floor and covered her mouth. Her shoulders heaved. This wasn't fair. All she wanted was to feel normal and yet she felt anything but.

After Jewel's mother had died, a piece of her died too. She cut everyone off. That included her father, brother and his fiancée at the time. She thought she could deal with the emotions on her own, but it had been over two years since she had seen any of them and they all lived within 30 minutes. She couldn't explain it—but her life just wasn't ready yet. She wasn't ready yet. She wanted so desperately to be, but every other day she was crying to herself on the floor or to sleep. A woman like that wasn't ready for anyone or anything. That's why she didn't deserve their love—she had nothing to give in return.

21

A Hidden Mess

It took Jewel several minutes to calm down. When she could finally breathe easily and her body stopped shaking, she checked the time using her phone. It was 12:25pm. She noticed her father had sent her a text message after she ended the call. She ignored it and put her phone away before she turned and re-entered the room. The detectives smiled kindly as she closed the door behind her.

"Sorry about that, gentlemen."

"Not a problem at all, Ms. Kennedy," Detective Banes motioned to the seat opposite the desk in front of them. Jewel approached with gnawing dread and sat down, clutching her purse at her side.

"I just had a call with my father. He confirmed that I did use to go there and I did go missing."

"For almost 24 hours, Ma'am," Detective Banes nodded.

Jewel forced a swallow and looked to the black and white photocopy on the table. "I don't know how I can help you though," she said softly.

"Well, it's just procedure that we talk with you about it. We're contacting every child that ever attended, even if the statute of limitations has passed."

"What are you looking for?" Jewel breathed.

"So far we have 12 counts of rape and even more for molestation charges." Jewel touched her heart at the news. "The daycare also received a lot of government aid and grants during the 25 years they were open. We're looking to find out when the operation turned south. How long had it been going on? And just how many were victims," the detective reached for the photocopy and looked it over briefly. "If molestation and rape occurred while the daycare was operating on government funds, then we can press additional charges against the owners."

"Aren't they in custody without bail right now?" Jewel asked. She had purposefully tried to ignore the reports as they came in regarding the trial, but it was difficult. She heard people talking about it on the streets downtown. It was everywhere: in the office, on the radio, and news headlines kept popping up in her desktop ticker. She really had to work hard to try and forget about it, but somehow she still managed to get the daily digest.

"The male is still in custody but not the wife," Detective Banes responded.

"she's being investigated as well, if she knew about her husband's actions and did nothing—well...." the other officer, Detective Jones spoke up. His voice was decisively higher pitched than his partner.

Jewel swallowed and nodded. "Well, if there's anything I can do, I'd love to help. But I don't remember a thing," she said again flatly.

Detective Banes nodded, and then motioned to his partner. Detective Jones lifted a square sheet of paper from his lap and pushed it towards Jewel.

"We have therapist that work with our department. This is the counseling group. Do you think you could give them a call? We cover the first five sessions."

Jewel took the paper and stared at the card. "Okay. I'll call right away," she nodded as she began to stand. Her mind still felt numb, but she no longer felt dizzy or like she was going to faint. She still didn't remember anything though.

The detectives escorted Jewel to the central waiting area. From there, she left the building and tried to walk calmly towards her car. She ended up running and by the time she shut the door, she was out of breath and on the verge of panicking again. She quickly selected Landra's number from the menu and held the phone to her ear. Landra answered on the first ring.

"How'd the meeting go? What'd they want?"

Jewel couldn't restrain herself from vomiting up the information she had just received. She told Landra about her father's phone call and how she felt like her life was slipping and she had no idea why. Eventually, Landra was able to soothe and calm her down from the tears that had made it difficult for her to speak again.

"Jewel, I want you to consider something," Landra had finally gotten her friend's attention. From the car seat, Jewel sniffed and wiped at her eyes. She hated all the tears. She didn't generally cry, not that much anyway, but lately, it seemed every time she turned around there were tears in her eyes, tears on her cheeks, on her sheets, on her journal pages. She absolutely hated it—it made her feel weak.

"What is it?" Jewel asked.

"I think you should start with the therapist. You have five full sessions for free. Don't think about what it would mean, just make an appointment and follow through."

Although she knew the suggestion was reasonable, it made Jewel angry. She didn't think she should have to see a therapist. There was simply no need. She was perfectly fine— well, not *perfectly* fine but she could be perfectly fine if she could just stop the visions and images from bothering her in her sleep. That's all she wanted. Jewel remembered the cry of the little girl in dark; she remembered the emptiness of the hidden room. Suddenly, she recalled the intense feelings of fear and pain that kept the little girl from crying out, from saying anything.

That little girl had nothing but darkness surrounding her. Occasionally, she had managed a weak cry, hoping that someone would answer her from the darkness, but no one ever answered her. She was just alone.

Jewel didn't know what that meant. Would seeing a therapist help that little girl out somehow? Jewel was positive it had something to do with Lexy. Maybe it was Lexy in the dark room, calling out for her mother while her great-grandfather had taken advantage of her.

"Are you listening to me, Jewel? Did you hear the second thing I had to say?"

"What?" Jewel shook her thoughts away. "I didn't hear you. I'm sorry," she said feebly.

She heard Landra take a deep breath from the other line. "I said I think you should call David and tell him about this. And your dream too—."

"No way," Jewel said quickly. "I've never told anyone about the dream except you. I can't do that."

"Jewel, please just listen to me," Landra said quickly. Jewel bit her lip to keep from interrupting again. "I don't understand your reasons for not opening up to David, okay? But please, just listen to me."

Jewel forced herself to nod. "I'm listening."

"I don't have trouble sleeping at night, Jewel," Landra began. "In fact, I have a great relationship with my parents and my siblings."

"What's your point?"

"You don't have these things, do you, Jewel?"

Jewel heaped a sigh. She knew where her friend was going with this.

"You frequently go through periods of insomnia. You've been having visions which have been affecting you at work, outside of work, your relationships—."

"What is your point, Landra?" Jewel's voice was harsher than she intended it. Landra didn't seem to take offense.

"My point is that if a client came to you with these...symptoms. Let's call them symptoms, okay? What's a symptom, Jewel?"

Her teeth were clenched again and she clutched the phone tightly. She hated it when Landra walked her through problems like these.

"Please answer the question, Jewel," Landra carried a professional calm in her voice. It was the therapist's voice.

With a heavy sigh and through gritted teeth, Jewel responded, "It's a sign of the existence of something."

When her friend spoke again, her voice was much softer, "Don't you want to know what that something is?" Landra asked. "I love you so, so much, Jewel. I can't stand to see you so down. You're so smart and successful. Don't you deserve to know what is causing all of this?"

Jewel's lip started to tremble. The idea of facing this, whatever *this* was, filled her with dread. Complete and utter dread. It made her body freeze and her throat close. She felt like she would suffocate.

"I'm just so scared," Jewel managed. She had never been able to voice it before. Forcing the words out brought a small moment of elation. Maybe she could get through this.

"I know, sweetie. But you have David. He can be your strength. He can help you—he wants to help you. Let him, Jewel. Call him. Please. If a client came to you with these symptoms, you would tell them they have to be explored. You would start with the dream, right?" Again, Jewel knew Landra was on to something.

"I've got to go. I have a client walking in my door right now— Thank you. Oh no, it's okay. Have a seat," Landra's voice had pulled away from the receiver. When she spoke again, her voice was loud, "I've got to go, sweetie. Call David."

Jewel nodded and ended the call. She resisted the urge to toss the phone into her purse. Landra would check on her later and would only be hurt if she didn't follow through. She navigated through the phone menu and selected David's number. Her hands had started shaking again. It was probably due to a lack of lunch.

"Jewel?" David answered the call quickly.

"David," her tone was less than happy. She felt David's energy shift immediately.

"What's wrong, Jewel?"

His question seemed so innocent, yet Jewel felt like she had to push through a brick wall to force herself to answer. "I need to eat lunch. I'm near the station. Can you meet me?"

"Sure thing."

Jewel didn't know how David managed to reserve his time for her. Probably because she rarely called him during the day, let alone request his presence during lunch. Either way, they selected a downtown deli, the one she and Landra loved to frequent, and made arrangements to meet there soon. After the phone call, Jewel lowered the phone and held up the paper with the counselor's information. She wasn't going to call that place. Not yet.

She stuffed the paper into her purse along with her phone and started the car. Her stomach jittered at the thought of telling David. She worried about what he would think of her if anything at all. Would he tell her she was ridiculous? How would he feel if she had to have counseling? Jewel shivered.

Men wanted strong women—women with a good head on their shoulders who weren't easily shaken. That wasn't Jewel right now. She felt weak, and perhaps a bit crazy. She couldn't explain her behavior or even some of her actions. All she knew is how to hide it, and even now she was slipping at being able to cover her hidden mess.

Jewel took a deep breath and tried to focus on the road. She let herself get immersed in driving and checked the license plates of passing cars. After a few stoplights, she switched on the radio and forced herself to sing along.

To her dismay, she saw David's car parked along the side of the café. He was still inside and smiled as he saw her pass in her vehicle. Forcing a smile in return, Jewel's body started to quake. Her insides felt jittery and her fingertips tingled. She told herself it was just low blood sugar. She searched the inside of her car for a bottle of water. Her mouth was suddenly dry. There wasn't any water in her car.

She decided that she would purchase a glass as soon as she was able to once she made it inside and found a parking space near the side entrance of the deli. David had chosen to sit outside, she mused as she parked.

"How fortunate," she grumbled beneath her breath. She didn't feel like eating outside where it was sunny and happy. She wanted to eat inside where it was cold and hopefully the atmosphere mirrored her feelings. Everything about the weather and the day was in stark contrast to her feelings and emotions. It all felt like a lie.

"I'm glad you called me," David said quickly as Jewel neared. She couldn't manage a smile this time.

She weakly gestured towards the table. "Thank you for meeting me," her voice was thin and tired.

David sat on the edge of his seat. "I have glasses of water coming," he watched Jewel sit and continued, "Landra called me after I spoke with you."

Jewel's eyes widened. She stared at David. "What did she tell you?"

"Everything," he said softly.

"Everything?" Oddly enough, Jewel felt the unease building within her subside. There was a flash of anger, and yet a steady sense of calm immediately rushed in to take its place. "My dreams?"

David nodded. "She said I should probably let you tell me, but I knew it would be difficult for you." A man stepped to the table and set down two glasses of water. Jewel reached for hers quickly. "A moment more before we order," David told the man quietly. He bowed his head and quietly turned away. David faced Jewel again.

"Is this why you shut me out?" He asked softly.

Jewel cleared her throat. David was never one to beat around the bush. Still, she had trouble meeting his eyes. She stared at the table, taking notice of her napkin instead. With difficulty, she found herself nodding her head in agreement.

"I'm scared," was all that she could manage. She took a deep breath and closed her eyes. She remembered the image of the little girl huddled in darkness. She could feel the fear, the pain. "I've had this same dream for so many years, so many nights. And then the news about the daycare. Did Landra tell you about that?" Jewel glanced towards David but looked away before he answered.

"Yes. She told me that you went missing, but you don't remember any of it."

Jewel nodded. "I should remember something like that, right?"

"Have you called the therapist yet?"

She cursed Landra silently. She didn't like all the questions, the accountability. Even so, she knew that was exactly why her friend called David. If it was left up to her, she knew there would have been a high chance that not all the information would have been properly relayed

Jewel shook her head and then reached for the glass of water. It was already half gone. She finished it and lowered it onto the moist napkin gently. She hadn't met David's eyes once.

"Are you going to?"

Shrugging her shoulders, Jewel looked around at the nearby tables. There was a woman eating alone, a couple, and what appeared to be two coworkers sharing a meal together. They seemed content for the moment, symptom-free of anything keeping them from enjoying life. Jewel took another deep breath and finally met David's gaze.

"I don't remember anything, David. Nothing," she shook her head. "I feel like it'd be a waste."

She watched David's face harden, but he remained silent. The man that had delivered the water returned again. They took the break in the conversation to order their meal. Jewel didn't feel hungry, but she ordered a Panini regardless. She was able to make breakfast that morning, but that was well over four hours ago.

"I think you should go to at least a few counseling session," David began again once the waiter had left their table.

Jewel frowned and shrugged. "I don't know," she paused, "I

might."

David watched Jewel carefully. "I just want to see you happy," he said softly. Jewel met his gaze.

"Me too," she admitted.

"Don't you think a therapist might be the first step towards that?"

Jewel drew air into her lungs and began to fidget with the napkin pinned beneath her empty water glass. "What if I don't want to remember what happened?"

David reached across the table and took hold of Jewel's hand. He held it, encircling his hands around hers. He simply kept it there. "I'll go with you," he said softly.

Jewel smiled. "You'd do that?" David nodded quickly.

"Of course I would. You know that."

Her smile brightened. She did know that. David was true to his word. He removed his hands and Jewel pushed her hair over her shoulders and gulped down another breath. Somehow, it didn't seem right that she would have come to know such an incredible man. She eyed him curiously. Her gaze made him smile.

"What? What are you thinking?"

Jewel chuckled. "Just that you're incredible," her smile faded. "I'm very lucky to have you."

David shook his head. "No, not lucky. You deserve everything I want to give you. You're a great woman."

Jewel sniffed. She didn't have anything more to say. She was never really good at receiving praise.

"So do you want me to come with you?"

Meeting David's eyes, Jewel's brief concern was replaced with comfort. She considered David's question and pushed the napkin around with the pad of her forefinger. "I don't know. I might be okay for the first meeting."

David smiled. "You're stronger than you realize, Jewel," he comforted.

She reached for him this time and stroked his skin when her hand met is. "Thank you for being here for me."

22

The Scrutiny of Another...

Jewel killed her car engine and surveyed the counseling building from her car. With David's presence, she made the appointment. The soonest that she could see Mr. Alura, the therapist, was in two days. It was 48 hours of hell.

Just as she predicted, the visions started to come back. It was the little girl again, innocently walking down the hall. The more Jewel contemplated the dreams and visions, the more she felt Lexy really looked like her. Lexy was bi-racial and had soft, brown curls like the little girl from the visions. Jewel was certain that they were connected, but she didn't know how to address the little girl about them.

She had seen Lexy the previous day. She learned that often times, the great grandfather made her touch him as well. Lexy said she didn't like that, but she always did it because she was scared. The thought of a grown man fondling a prepubescent girl was sickening.

169

Jewel was used to these types of stories, the realities where innocent women had been violated. They were almost always by someone they knew. A close friend, a coworker. She even had a young woman near the beginning of the year who had been raped by a family member. These women were violated, scared into silence, and forced to submit themselves to the terrible torture.

She helped so many find healing, but little Lexy was different. Jewel felt like she would be able to help the child in the long run, but she also feared that she wouldn't be able to. It was a foreign feeling for her to doubt herself. She had an unusual confidence in dealing with young women who had been violated. Even young teens, but Lexy was the first case of someone so young who had come into her office. Perhaps it was the dream of Lexy that prevented her from doing her work. Jewel couldn't be too sure, but her heart was too raw when Lexy was in her presence. It was like she could also *feel* her pain.

She saw her innocence peeking through their role play when she opted to be princess and play act with Barbie dolls. It didn't make sense to her why someone would ruin, or try to ruin, such a sweet life. But she already knew the answer. This had nothing to do with Lexy and everything to do with her terrible great grandfather, and those that permitted the abuse.

This is what happened when victims failed to get treatment for themselves. They usually ended up permitting the cycle of abuse to continue. Jewel knew that some women didn't know what options were available. They were too scared to seek them out. What angered her more than anything were the women that sought for help and were turned away or shamed into letting the abuse continue even more.

This was the world that she saw on a daily basis. She

understood how it was often easier for people to pretend that it didn't exist. It was so much easier to enjoy a perfect day when you didn't have to face the reality that others faced: the fears and scars that women were experiencing even now, as Jewel sat in her car.

That was probably the hardest part for Jewel. Years ago when she first came into the business, she began to realize that there would only be so many she would be able to protect and help. She realized that even with a full case load from the state, the courts, or individuals seeking their own intensive healing, there would always be hundreds or thousands more who would never see the breaking dawn of hope and restoration in their lives. They would be trapped, and they would lead others to feeling the same.

Jewel's phone began to ring. It was David. She answered with a meek voice.

"Hey, David."

"Are you there?" David asked immediately. She smiled. Some days she really loved his eagerness and ability to skip the chitchat to get straight to the point. Today, however, she really wasn't too fond of it. He promised her he would call five minutes before the appointment to give her last minute strength with a prayer for the session. Jewel was happy he called.

"Yes, I'm still in my car parked outside. I was waiting for your call," that last part wasn't exactly the truth. She hadn't been *waiting* for David per se, but she had been waiting. Probably for her own strength and resolve to arrive. They hadn't yet, but she was still a bit warmed to hear David's voice.

"I want to pray for you," David said solemnly. "Will you let me do that for you?"

Jewel smiled and leaned against the back of her seat. She closed her eyes. "Of course. You're always welcome to pray over me."

"Okay," David took in a breath. "Dear Heavenly Father, I come before you now with your precious daughter, Jewel. You know her heart, Father. You know her strengths and her weaknesses. You know that she is scared," Jewel shifted at his words, "Lord, please give her strength to confront what she fears most. Give her strength to dive into what she has tried to forget. Help her, Lord, to move forward with success and victory. Help her, Father, to know peace. I ask all of this in Jesus', holy and wonderful name. Amen."

Jewel muttered into the phone, "Amen." She and David had frequented church together often, it was refreshing to have him pray for her. "What a prayer," she grumbled, not knowing what else to say.

David chuckled on the other line. "I meant every word of it. He can heal you, Jewel. You just have to ask."

She was scowling now. She didn't think fixing her life was a matter of a simple request. "Thank you, sweetie," she tried to force the agitation out of her. She wasn't sure if it worked or not, but David didn't comment on it.

"It's about time for you to get going in there, Jewel. I'll still be praying for you."

She nodded and slipped out the car. Jewel shouldered her purse as she locked the door. "Thank you, baby. I'll call you when I'm out," she said goodbye and ended the phone call. As she approached the building, she pushed her phone into her purse and caught a glimpse of her reflection in the glass panes of the front door.

Her hair was wild and gorgeous, her eyes sharp and dark. She wore a fitting pair of dark slacks and a flowing floral blouse that complimented her figure well. In that split second her reflection called out to her and reminded her of how many people so often said she was beautiful. Jewel didn't feel it in her core. Inside her heart, she felt like a broken, empty vessel of a shell whose only hope was to help other women. She didn't know who could actually help her in return.

Inside, a stellar office greeted her. A receptionist behind glass took her name and handed her a clipboard of intake paperwork. Jewel frowned when she saw the stack, but she knew the routine. Taking a pen, she sat down and let herself relax in the ambient décor and atmosphere of the room.

The first page was the fee schedule that followed the five free sessions covered by the state. She lifted it and tucked it beneath the clipboard so that she could begin to fill out the client information section with her name, address, employer, emergency contact information and basic health and medical coverage information.

She numbly went through the process of selecting the best time frames for appointments and froze when she turned the page over. It was a symptom assessment. She looked at the page and then read it twice. She needed to select how often she experienced worry or tension, intense fear, feelings of guilt, panic attacks, recurring or distressing thoughts about an event. Jewel stopped reading the list. She decided to skip that section and continued to a second area on the same page about personal and family mental health history.

All of it made her stomach sink. Just the words "mental health" rubbed Jewel the wrong way. She always told her clients that they were so brave for taking the first step and admitting that they needed help. She commended them for seeking a way to find healing, but Jewel didn't feel like that applied to her. She actually felt a little forced. It didn't seem right for a therapist to seek "mental health" help. That made her sound like her life was out of control. But wasn't it out of control?

"No," Jewel said out loud. She paused and lifted her eyes from the clipboard of papers. She was the only one in the room. Still, she bit her lip and reprimanded herself. She couldn't be seen talking to herself in the waiting room of a counseling clinic. Someone might think she actually belonged there, or somewhere else. The thought made the hair on her skin stand and dance.

After the short second on past family mental health, there was another assessment group of questions about her job, significant relationships, family relationships, and general happiness and other relationship related questions. With another frown, Jewel skipped that section as well. She wasn't here for herself, she decided. She was here for the cops. They suggested she come. If it could help Lexy, then she was all for it. But those questions didn't have anything to do with her.

The next page was for statistical purposes. Jewel circled her occupation, location within the city, highest education level along with her income, ethnicity, and employment category. Next was the consent to treatment forms. She skimmed it easily. All counseling consent forms were more or less the same. She began to hum as her eyes danced along the lines of the black ink on the page and she signed and dated where needed. Finally, the torture was over.

She sat the clipboard down and breathed out relief. In 50 minutes, she would likely be on her way without any information regarding her visions. Oddly enough, she felt like that thought comforted her. She vaguely recalled that the dreams and visions were interrupting her sleep cycles and frowned at the previous thought. Didn't she want to visions and dreams to stop? That's why she was here. She was hoping for revelation regarding those painful glimpses of something she was sure was Lexy's miserable reality.

She didn't know how she could end up catching a glimpse into another's personal traumatic time in their life, but it was happening. Now she just had to figure out how to use the visions to help Lexy. That was why she was really here. Understanding the visions meant she could help Lexy somehow.

Within several minutes, a tall peach-toned man in casual attire emerged from within the hallway of the building. Jewel eyed him carefully. Was that Mr. Alura? He had peppered hair and broad shoulders but soft, blue eyes. He stopped just a few steps from the hallway for a drink of water from the water fountain. When he stood, he turned and met Jewel's eyes directly. After a second, he flashed is brilliant teeth in a dazzling smile.

"Good afternoon, I'm Mr. Alura."

Jewel took the man in silently. His kind eyes somehow seemed familiar to her. "Jewel," she cleared her throat. "I'm Jewel Kennedy, Mr. Alura," she stood and stretched out her hand. When he took it, she remembered. "I ran into you over a week ago. At the cemetery, remember? Was that you?"

Mr. Alura pursed his lips as he contemplated Jewel's claim. He took her in with a renewed interest. A smile slowly returned to his face. "I do believe you're correct, Ms. Kennedy."

"Oh please, call me Jewel," she said softly. She turned and reached for the clipboard. "I've finished the intake."

He took the board from her and motioned her to join him in the back. Once they settled into seats within a stuffy counseling room, Jewel took a deep breath and tried to relax against the cushions of the loveseat. There wasn't much in the room, just a sparsely decorated bookshelf, coffee table, and two end tables with lamps. There was also a short desk and a recliner that Mr. Alura claimed.

Jewel sat in silence as he looked over the papers. He flipped two pages and frowned.

"I see that you didn't complete the assessment," he said softly.

Jewel arched her back and broke their eye contact briefly. "Well, I'm only here because the police station suggested I come to help with their investigation," she paused. Mr. Alura's expression carried kind interest. "I just didn't think the assessments applied to me directly."

He nodded. "Yes, I have had contact with the station. They informed me of your situation. You once attended the daycare," he paused and nodded, looking for acknowledgment.

"Yes, that's right."

Mr. Alura nodded again. "Well, it helps me better serve my clients to have even a little of the assessments complete, so," his voice lingered, "if you don't mind, I'd like to just take you through some verbally."

Jewel resisted the urge to sigh and roll her eyes. She forced a tight-lipped smile and agreed with a nod. "Sure thing. I'll let you do your job. I know the routine."

Mr. Alura began at the beginning of the pages she skipped. He asked her about worry, tension, and fear. Jewel responded with having seldom experienced many of the situations until he asked about guilt. She hesitated at the question, causing Mr. Alura to raise his eyes to connect with hers.

"About how often would you say you experience feelings of guilt?"

Jewel frowned. She always felt guilty. "What type of guilt? I mean, guilt for what?"

He lowered the clipboard and crossed his legs like a middle-aged professional. "Guilt for anything," he said quietly. "Do you feel guilt often? We can talk about why you feel the guilt later."

Jewel hesitantly admitted to experiencing feelings of guilt often. Mr. Alura moved on to ask about panic attacks. Jewel was about to say seldom but stopped as he continued speaking.

"Trembling, shortness of breath, sweating, shaking palms that you can't stop. Things like that for a panic attack," he looked up from the clipboard. "Have you ever experienced something like that?" He glanced at the sheet. "Oh, I forgot heart palpitations."

Jewel shifted again, "Well, I have experienced some of those things."

Mr. Alura raised an inquisitive brow. "Oh? Would you mind explaining?"

With a deep breath, Jewel wrung her hands together in her lap. "Sometimes I get dizzy," she began with caution. "It usually happens when I see something, like a vision. Sometimes I have visions."

Mr. Alura began to write on her paperwork. His eyes never looked down to the sheet. He kept his gaze steady with Jewel's. "Tell me more," he urged. "What do you see?"

Jewel pressed her lips together. "I see a little girl," she heaved a breath and forced herself to continue. "The little girl sees something awful."

Mr. Alura nodded. "Do you know the girl?"

Jewel shook her head. "Sometimes I have dreams. When I see the visions, it usually makes me pass out or something. The feelings are so real to me. So intense."

"You feel with these visions?" Mr. Alura stopped writing.

With an eager nod, Jewel said, "Yes. I see it like a movie, but then I feel it like it's me."

He nodded. "Would you call these periods blackouts?"

"Yes," she agreed readily.

"When you black out, what happens?"

"Um, I don't know. It's hard to explain," Jewel admitted with a sigh. It was incredibly easy to speak with Mr. Alura. He seemed to know exactly what she was experiencing. His questions weren't out of an odd curiosity, but one of strict concern. "I know that I do struggle with memory loss, though."

"And can you tell me about the feelings you experience?"

Jewel chuckled and locked several curls behind her ear. "Well, it is very odd. I think I cry in my sleep sometimes. Then there's the fear," Jewel swallowed at the thought. "The little girl's fear is overwhelming. Sometimes paralyzing," she paused for a moment, "I met a little girl not too long ago. She's the great-granddaughter of the old man who owned the daycare. Her name is Lexy and I think these visions are about her," she said in a breath. "I don't know why or how, but I think if I can figure these dreams out, I might be able to help her."

Mr. Alura had long ago stopped writing. He sat the clipboard down and uncrossed his legs. "You believe these visions are a unique gift for Lexy?

Jewel nodded. "I never understood them until I met her. She looks just like the little girl from my dreams."

"How long have you had these visions?"

"Years," Jewel nearly whispered.

Mr. Alura nodded solemnly. "So what do you think of the situation at the station?"

Confusion overtook Jewel. "You mean about me having attended the daycare?"

He nodded. "Just tell me your thoughts."

Jewel shrugged. "I think there has to be a mistake or something."

Mr. Alura gave a sure nod. "Hmm. I'd like to meet with you in a couple of days, if that's okay, Ms. Kennedy."

With a frown, Jewel responded, "I just don't understand what I have to do with the daycare."

He seemed to contemplate Jewel's words. "Well, if your visions can shed light into Lexy, don't you think they're worth exploring?"

"Absolutely," Jewel said quickly.

Mr. Alura agreed. "Then I think I would prefer another meeting with you. My secretary will be in touch about the date and time. We're going to get to the bottom of this, Ms. Kennedy."

Jewel felt her mouth beginning to dry. She had never been

subject to the scrutiny of another therapist before. She wasn't sure she liked the experience, but it was becoming apparent to her that Mr. Alura was a seasoned teacher in the field.

She didn't know what else to say to Mr. Alura, so she merely nodded.

23
Past Secrets Revealed

It was Monday of the following week when Jewel received the call from Mr. Alura's office. It was something she had silently been dreading. The visions had come and gone in their usual rounds in between that time, disrupting her sleep and making it difficult to focus.

David had grown more curious about them, but Jewel remained silent to the option of only discussing the visions. It was one thing for a trained professional to inquire about them. He knew what he was doing. She didn't feel like explaining to David everything again. Jewel knew just from speaking with Mr. Alura that he understood what she meant when she felt the pain as if it were her own. David would have needed further explanation.

He'd want to know about her crying. He'd ask her to call him; he'd be in—in too deep for her. The feelings were fresh. It was like they weren't meant for others to know about. If it was Lexy's pain, it wasn't worth sharing for curiosity's sake.

She felt Lexy needed to be protected. She knew the little girl would have to be helped through her feelings to process everything. She had seen her the past Friday. Lexy smiled and giggled, but when it came time to talk about how her great grandfather had touched her, her face emptied and she wrapped her hands around her body protectively. She wasn't ready.

Lexy had confided in Jewel that she was happy the old man was gone, but she said she felt angry. She also felt alone and sad. Just like the little girl in her visions. Jewel was convinced more than ever that they were helping her to understand Lexy more. If she had been handed the case before this time, Jewel might not have been able to help her.

Jewel wasn't entirely sure if she were ready for the call from Mr. Alura's secretary, but it came nevertheless. However, the call wasn't about making another appointment time. The secretary called with a time and a location for Jewel. That part seemed a little odd to her. She had never known about counselors meeting clients outside of their office. She wasn't sure of what to expect.

She put the address into her phone's GPS and set it to display hands-free while driving. A friendly British female voice kindly directed her through Illinois, off the highway and into dense family neighborhoods. It was turning out to be a pleasant drive until Jewel suddenly realized she was near her old home. The thought pricked her curiosity.

She hadn't been on this side of town in ages, it seemed. A smile tugged at Jewel's lips and she checked the time. Her appointment was at 1:30pm, at the tail end of her lunch. She still had twenty minutes to arrive and she was actually on time. Jewel decided to detour and head to the last home where her mother stayed while she was healthy.

Her cancer had come on quickly. By the time it was discovered, she was already at Stage 3 with an extremely aggressive type of cancer. Surgery didn't help and it had been decided that chemo or radiation was only likely to make her weaker. Her survival rate was less than twenty percent. After surgery, they didn't try any more treatment options.

Jewel turned down the old, familiar street and took a deep breath in. Although her windows were sealed and she technically breathed the conditioned air of her Prius, she felt like the air was cleaner here, more innocent. She remembered Christmas mornings with her brother, a Christmas tree full of lights and a kitchen full of cookies, milk, presents and heating food for the evening dinner.

Christmas at her house was always loud. Friends and family stopped by at all times of the day. Their door was constantly revolving and the entire Christmas time was filled with laughs, good times, and great memories. Jewel remembered laughing a lot as a little girl. Her mother loved styling her hair and usually changed the style every couple of days or so. She loved that time she had spent with her mother, nestled in her lap while her mother decided a new way to present her daughter.

Her father had been a lot happier back then too—they had all been happier. They smiled and laughed more. With a frown, Jewel slowed the car outside the old familiar home. Eventually, she came to a complete stop and just looked. She wondered what happened to her family. What happened to the love?

She remembered her father's warm voice over the phone at the police station. He was a good dad; he would always be there for her, but it seemed like there was something holding them all back from reaching their true potential with one another. She and Keith had drifted apart. He stopped calling her over a year ago. She still loved her big brother deeply, but there was something keeping her from being able to commit fully to the strength of their relationship. Whatever it was kept her from rebuilding the relationship with her father as well.

Jewel was staring out the glass of the driver's side window before she noticed that there was a car in the driveway of the old home. She eyed the vehicle curiously, and then realized someone was watching her from the living room of the house. She faintly saw the outline of their body behind the blinds but saw the separation in the blinds where the hidden individual peered out at her. Jewel put the Prius in drive and began to pull away.

The GPS recalculated the route and had her make a U-turn at the end of the cul-de-sac to correct the course. She followed the directions and took her time and let herself take in each of the houses on the block. She vaguely remembered the friends to whom the homes had belonged. As she prepared to pull out of the street into the main road, she felt an odd feeling of familiarity creep over her. She had traveled this path before.

The phone directions instructed her to remain on the main street for several lights before turning onto another small road which entered another neighborhood in the suburbs of the greater Chicago area. Jewel slowed the speed of her vehicle significantly as she turned onto the road and took each home in accordingly. This way seemed very familiar to her, yet she knew she had never driven it before. It had been years, nearly ten since she had come to this side of town.

With impending dread, Jewel *knew* the destination home before she saw the address numbers painted on the wooden beams on the front porch. The front lawn was a dying shade of yellow grass and there was a rusted entrance to a backyard around the side of the house.

Mr. Alura stood on the front porch and smiled when he and Jewel made eye contact. He was still adorned in business casual attire but seemed so much more sophisticated than his simple slacks and collared shirt with a tie would have suggested.

Dread gnawed at Jewel as she stepped out of the car. The old, worn home was so familiar, even down to the grass on the front lawn. Her head began to buzz again with a sickly tapping on the edge of her conscious. She didn't want to cross the width of her car to the old concrete path that led to the front porch, but she forced her legs to move. With each step, they seemed to fill with lead, bogging her down.

A wave of heat rushed over her and Jewel reached her forehead to wipe. When she brought it down, she saw a streak of sweat across the back of her hand. When did she start sweating? It wasn't even hot outside. The sun was out and shining, but it was fall and a cool breeze was in the air. Her armpits itched as her body grew hot and uncomfortable. Mr. Alura watched her carefully.

"Are you okay?" He called out to her.

Jewel stopped walking. Everything in her body was telling her to head back to her car. She looked at the outside of the house again and her face twisted in disgust.

She finally shook her head. "Why have you asked me to come here? What is this place?"

"This is the daycare," Mr. Alura responded calmly. "It's A Small World, do you remember this place?"

Jewels lips and hands trembled. She looked down at her feet, and then around at the grass on either side of the concrete path. She couldn't speak. Mr. Alura stepped down from the porch and made his way to Jewel.

"What are you feeling right now, Jewel? You seem really upset."

Jewel could only nod. "I don't want to be here," she admitted. Mr. Alura took hold of her hand gently.

"I'd like you to come inside with me. Do you think you can do that?"

No. She didn't want to do that. He took a step forward, but Jewel yanked her hand back and even took a step away. He stopped and turned to her.

"Talk to me about what you're feeling," his voice was quiet and soothing.

Jewel struggled to swallow back the tack that was forming in her mouth. She was suddenly thirsty. She needed water. "I don't know," she hesitated, her head swelling with too many thoughts. She touched her chest, groping for her heart. "I'm scared," she choked out.

Mr. Alura joined Jewel at her side and slowly took her hand again. The gentle action made Jewel look into his eyes. "That's right. Just look at me. I want to show you something." She didn't realize when they had started walking. "So you feel scared. Is that right?"

Jewel began to look to her side, but Mr. Alura pulled her eyes back to his with a command, "Just look at me. Don't look around. We're going to step up to the front porch, okay? Can you tell me what you feel?"

"Fear," she answered. A tear escaped her eye. She wasn't even sure when they had begun to water. They were at the front porch. Mr. Alura took a step up and then helped Jewel take a step. They were right in front of the door.

"How does that fear make you feel?" He asked her calmly. He turned and knocked on the door; but, instead of waiting for an answer, he turned the knob and pushed it open. Before Jewel could speak, he was talking to her again and slowly drew her into the house. "It's a little hot outside. Do you mind if we step in?"

Jewel shook her head as an answer, but she meant to say, "Yes." She didn't want to go inside, but they were, and Mr. Alura shut the door behind them. "Just keep talking to me, Jewel. Walk me through your feelings."

"I feel alone," she whimpered. Mr. Alura nodded. She noticed a figure standing behind him near the far back wall of the main room. There was an older woman there. She had to be in her late sixties. Jewel frowned. She had met this woman before. "Who is that?" Jewel asked in a breath.

"This is Ms. Fuller. This was her daycare. It's been shut down while the investigation ensures."

Jewel found herself curiously examining the old woman. When their eyes met, she looked down and clasped her hands tightly in front of her.

"What are you feeling, Jewel? Can you tell me what you're thinking?"

"She looks familiar. Have we met?" Jewel asked, full curiosity taking over. Her voice found strength. The older woman didn't answer.

"Thank you, Ma'am, for allowing me to bring my client here," Mr. Alura addressed Ms. Fuller, but she didn't lift her head or say a word. She just stood silently, with her head down and her hands intertwining tightly.

There was a noise down a hallway to the left of the front room. Jewel looked to the sound and saw a younger woman emerge. She was Lexy's mother. When they noticed each other, time seemed to freeze.

"What are you doing here?" Lexy's mother asked. She walked towards them and entered the room, glancing towards Ms. Fuller, and then towards Jewel. At length, she met Mr. Alura.

"Who are you?" She asked with interest.

"I'm Mr. Alura, a therapist with the Chicago Therapist Counseling Group. We work with police station victims in traumatic care for adults. Your grandmother agreed to let me bring a client here for a therapy session."

Lexy's mother snorted. "Some place for a session," she turned to Jewel and jerked her head to Jewel. "Did you used to come here?" Her questions and voice grated on Jewel's ear like violating assaults from a cannon. "Did your children come here?"

Jewel shook her head, unable to stop her face from showing disgust. "I don't have kids."

Mr. Alura interjected. "Jewel once attended 22 years ago."

Lexy's mother's eyes widened. Her eyes darted between Ms. Fuller and Jewel. "You came here as a little girl?"

Jewel shook her head, and Mr. Alura interceded to answer for her. "Yes. For about three months while she was six. She goes by the name Jewel but her birth name is Julianna. Do you remember a Julianna Kennedy, Ms. Fuller?" The older woman barely moved her head. Her mouth was glued shut. "This is the little girl that went missing from here about a year after the daycare opened."

Lexy's mother's gasped and grabbed her mouth. She glanced at Jewel and Ms. Fuller. "Grandma, this is the little girl," she breathed. She stepped towards Jewel.

"Do you remember me?" The mother asked.

Jewel choked on a breath. She couldn't answer. Instead, she said, "I didn't go missing. There's a mistake with that."

The mother nodded her head eagerly. "Yes, you did. You did go missing. I was with you. I'm Samantha. Do you remember?" She looked towards Mr. Alura. "How does she not remember?" Silence fell on the room like a thick, wool blanket. Jewel tried to back away, but her hand was still firmly enclosed in Mr. Alura's grasp. He turned to her then.

"Tell me what you're feeling, Jewel," he said softly. His voice grounded Jewel back in reality. She met his eyes like a wild gazelle, fleeting and darting to and fro, but she couldn't say anything. Her voice was gone.

"Come here and follow me," Samantha instructed. She urged Mr. Alura to follow her down the corridor she had just emerged from. There was a door on the right and another on the left near the end before it reached a pair of stairs that led to the next floor. Samantha stopped at the door on the left and opened it. She looked into the room, and then turned and held a hand out for Mr. Alura and Jewel to enter first.

"Can you tell me what you're feeling?" He asked with a soft and comforting voice. He moved towards the door, holding Jewel's gaze steady and he gently coaxed her forward.

"I don't know. I don't like it, whatever it is," she finally managed. She felt like her heart would explode. At the doorway to the room, Jewel forced her eyes to look in first. She stopped breathing. "The stairs," she choked. "The stairs," she repeated.

Mr. Alura nodded. "Do you remember these?"

"My dream," she spoke in chopped chunks of sound.

"Do you want to walk through?" Mr. Alura asked. He touched Jewel's back.

Curiously, she touched the doorknob, just as the little girl had. She suddenly remembered the anticipation the little girl from her dream had.

"She was hiding from something," Jewel said in a death whisper. She wasn't even sure anyone had heard her. Jewel dragged her hands along the railing of the stairs as she descended a step. "She came in here to hide. They were playing hide and go seek," Jewel took more steps. Here, she paused, remembering the dream vividly. "There was something that didn't fit. A sound. The lights were on down here," Jewel pointed at the bottom of the stairs. "The girl heard a sound, like a whine. A muffled whine," she swallowed back and continued down the stairs. After three more steps, she removed her hand from the railing, just as the little girl had done.

"She was scared," she recounted. "She wanted to turn away, but then she remembered she was still playing the game and she didn't know what the sound was. She continued down the stairs." Jewel took the steps slowly, as if she were the little girl, pensively moving towards the end of the darkened staircase.

She didn't hear the breathing and footsteps and Mr. Alura and

Samantha following her. Instead, all she saw was the dream in front of her eyes, playing like a tape overlaying her retinas. As they reached the bottom of the steps, Jewel turned, just as the little girl had and froze. She pointed through the darkness towards the back wall.

"This is where she saw it. The little girl," she gasped. "A man. An old man. He was standing in front of a bed, or cot. There was a little girl in front of him."

At the bottom of the stairs, Samantha reached for a light switch behind Mr. Alura's sturdy frame along the wall. Jewel didn't seem to be affected by the sudden change in light. In her mind, the lights were already on.

"He heard the girl, she made a noise. He turned and was angry. Furious." Jewel looked around the room curiously, but she didn't see the place as it was at present. Instead, she saw the room in a jagged blur of colors as the young girl from her dream had looked around, hopeless, searching for her mother, searching for anyone who might be able to save her.

"She peed herself," Jewel looked down at the floor. "She was so scared. He was so angry, she couldn't help it. The pee just ran down her leg and then she was so embarrassed," Jewel looked to the back wall again. "The girl on the bed was naked. Her clothes were completely gone, and she had tears all over her face—and then the man," Jewel pointed towards the man approaching the little girl. "He grabbed her by her hair. He was so strong. He completely picked her up, but the girl didn't scream, she couldn't."

Jewel turned completely, her eyes wide as she took in the old, familiar scene of the dream she had been having for years. "She's crying," Jewel whispered softly. "She was crying, and the man told her shut up. He hit her, and then he tossed her into a room, threw her on the ground where she puked."

After turning, Jewel pointed towards the rightmost wall where an empty, rickety metal shelf stood. In her vision, the rack was placed to the side of the door.

"That's the room where my grandfather used to hide me. That's where he hid her," Samantha said plainly. She motioned for Mr. Alura to help her move the shelf while Jewel stood and looked around in awe.

"I see it all," Jewel said softly. "There," she pointed to the room again. "He put her in there where there weren't any windows and there wasn't a light. Just a bed that the little girl didn't even know was there. He tossed her in." Samantha opened the door and turned to face Jewel as she passed and entered the room.

"She didn't know what time it was. She didn't know anything." Her eyes washed over the plain walls of the small concrete storm shelter. "At one point, another little girl was thrown into the room with her. The second girl gave the first a sandwich and a little bit of water. That's all she had while she was here. She was so hungry. She was so cold. So frightened and so alone," Jewel instinctively crossed her arms. Her brows were knitted tightly along her forehead.

"And then when the second little girl was taken away, he came back for the first one. He took her clothes off and he touched her," tears were on Jewel's face. She remembered everything about the dark little, room. The feelings of disgust and of complete and utter sheer terror. It was all coming back to her. "He made her put her clothes on when he was finished with her, and she never made a sound because she was so scared he'd beat her like he did that other little girl. She put her clothes on and laid on the bed like he told her too and didn't move."

A sob caught in Jewel's throat and she covered her mouth, muffling her own cries that had started to flow freely. "And then the door opened. Light came in and a woman told her to get up and to follow her. She was scared, but she did what she was told," Jewel turned around, staring through Mr. Alura's blue eyes. "They ran through the house into a car parked outside. The little girl pointed out her house and she was told to never go back to the daycare. To never talk about what happened. To never say anything to anyone. Ever." Mr. Alura's eyes came into focus. Jewel suddenly realized his presence. She noticed Samantha next. Her eyes were wet and moist. She sniffed.

"Jewel, that was you," Samantha whispered. "That little girl that you saw. That was me," Samantha's lips trembled. "My grandfather had raped me for months before that and then years afterward. Even after my mother died and I came to stay with them permanently. My grandmother," she pointed towards the ceiling. "Ms. Ella as the little girls called her," her voice cracked, "he beat her so bad for taking you home that day. He broke her collarbone, and her ribs," her voice became nearly indiscernible. "She was so scared she stopped talking except to me and the little kids. She couldn't do anything else but care for the children, but she could never stop him."

Jewel blinked at Samantha's words. She looked to Mr. Alura, and then around herself. Her eyes bounced around the room as if noticing it for the first time. She faced Mr. Alura again.

"How do you feel, Jewel?" He asked her softly.

Jewel stared at him momentarily and then faced Samantha. "You were the little girl in my dream?" Her words slurred together, thick and clouded with confusion.

Samantha nodded. "And you were the little girl he kidnaped." She pointed to the staircase. "He had just finished," she paused, "he had just finished raping me when you came down those stairs. He snatched you up and smacked you in the face. My grandmother was in the hospital for four days because she helped you home."

Jewel shook her head. "No."

Samantha nodded, equally as persistent. "Yes. I remember you. I gave you the bologna sandwich, remember?"

Gripping her heart, Jewel backed towards the staircase. "No!" She shouted, the sound ripping through the air like a loosed arrow.

Mr. Alura reached for Jewel.

"NO!" Jewel turned and rushed for the staircase. She took them two at a time and felt her vision blurring as she reached the top of the stairs. She started coughing, tears so thick in her eyes that she could hardly see.

Ms. Fuller was in the hallway. When Jewel burst through the door, she gasped. Her face was tear streaked.

"I'm so sorry, Julianna," she croaked. "I'm so sorry I couldn't save you," she collapsed into a puddle of tears. Mr. Alura and Samantha broke from the room seconds later, but Jewel was already in the lounge of the empty daycare. She paused briefly before she opened the front door and caught Mr. Alura's eyes.

"Please, come back Jewel. Let me help you."

Jewel just shook her head. She couldn't think—didn't feel, couldn't feel. She fled from the house and towards her car. She was already on the expressway before she realized she had no idea where she was driving, or which exit she had taken. She pulled the car onto the shoulder, her body overcome with a wave of fresh, tender pain. That little girl couldn't have been her, but at the same time, she knew it was.

All those dreams, all those memories, they were hers. When she was six years old, a grown man had penetrated her, stole her innocence, and took her life. Jewel's fingers scrambled for the passenger's side door. She did her best to lean over the middle console and armrest as bile and vomit climbed out of her throat. Only half made it outside and on the loose pebbles of the concrete shoulder. The rest clung tightly to the door, frame and foot rests. She continued to heave and vomit, relieved that for the moment, the pain in her gut took away from the pain and shock she felt in her heart.

24
Dirty & Forsaken

Jewel wasn't sure what time she finally managed to navigate her car through traffic towards her apartment. At some point, however, the familiar sight of her apartment building greeted her sore, tired eyes. She parked her car within the garage and moved throughout the building mindlessly. Inside her unit, she dropped her purse at the door and walked straight to her bed, letting her body sink into the covers. She didn't want to think. She didn't want to feel.

She cried herself to sleep. When she awoke, her body felt empty. When she closed her eyes, she saw the little girl. She felt the fright of having that man—that dirty, disgusting man—put his body next to hers, his weight on top of her—she puked several more times. There was nothing but bile left.

At some point, she managed to drink water and close the curtains. They let in too much light to remain open. The brightness seemed to burn her eyes and make her cry even more. She could smell herself after several days. She hadn't even brushed her teeth or taken the time to comb out her hair.

Every time she closed her eyes, she saw that frightened little girl; and, every time she realized it was her, she ached even more. She felt anger. Why hadn't anyone done something? How come no one told her?

With the curtains drawn and her mind muted, Jewel had no recollection of when a day started or ended. She vaguely heard her home phone ring in the distance. She turned it off; it hurt her ears too much. Her cellphone had long since died. She was completely isolated, completely alone. Just like the little girl.

Empty and formless thoughts inhabited her mind. Her father's words echoed in her ears. *"You never told us what happened..."* Vaguely, she wondered what he would think if he knew. Would she still be her father's sweet baby girl? She didn't feel like one.

She felt dirty and forsaken, soiled and hollow inside. With a gentle moan, she curled herself into the sheets and comforter on her bed. The dreams had finally stopped, but it seemed her living nightmare had just begun.

It took Jewel a moment to realize when she awoke that she was staring into David's eyes. He was crouched in front of her, his face level with her bed. She felt his hand on her back. Slowly, she rose and blinked, confused.

"What are you doing?" Her throat was so dry it hurt to speak. Her voice couldn't even properly manifest and only a scratchy whisper was heard.

"I've called for you for days," he said softly. "I got management to open the door. I told them you haven't left your room and we were scared."

"We?"

David nodded. "Landra's been here too. It's just me right now," he rubbed her back. "I know everything, Jewel."

Her gaze fell. She felt exposed. She tried to pull the sheets towards her, to cover herself, but David stopped her. He cupped the side of her face.

"I'm here," he whispered. Jewel watched him carefully. There were no expectations. No disappointment. Just love and care. Her lips trembled and David smiled at her. "It's okay, baby. I'm here," he pulled her into his chest. She heaved a cry and let the sobs overtake her. They didn't feel so helpless falling from her eyes as they had during the previous days before. Instead, she felt a cleansing move across her body as she cried this time, held securely in David's arms.

He spoke to her softly and rocked her body, encouraging her to cry while he whispered to her that she wasn't alone anymore.

"I'm right here, Jewel."

Was that true? Could she rise from being the little girl in the darkened room who had fear so great that she couldn't even speak?

David held and rocked Jewel long after her sobbing had ceased. She had even fallen asleep on his shoulder again. He lowered her down to her bed and she only stirred, nuzzling her face into the sheets and blankets even more.

When Jewel awoke, there was brightness in her room. Her eyes ached and burned; she shielded them with a hand and looked around. It was considerably cleaner than when she had fallen asleep. The air was no longer stale and she smelled the faint scent of cooking food wafting to her from the kitchen.

She pushed into the bathroom and marveled. There was no mistaking it now, someone had cleaned around her while she slept. The clothes she had strewn about were gone and she could see the counters again. The vomit she had left in the sink had been cleaned away. That last thought made her cringe. She wasn't a slob, but aside from water and dry bread, she hadn't been able to do much more for herself.

Jewel moved slowly and turned on the faucet. The water seemed much colder than she remembered. She let the cold liquid pool in her hands. With a flicker of movement, she splashed it onto her face. It stung, but it was surprisingly refreshing. She splashed more water on her face and then reached for her toothbrush. It was the first act of personal hygiene that she had taken in days.

After her teeth had been brushed, she considered a shower. Her body was weak. She didn't think she could stand for that long. Instead, she reached for a towel and used it to wash up. She changed her clothes and slipped into a loose pair of shorts and a tank. Her hair was much too unruly with the lack of proper care, so she decided to pull it into a sloppy ponytail knowing she would still look better than she had just a few days previously.

She left her bedroom tentatively and peered into the kitchen from the hallway, expecting to see David. Instead, Landra was at her stovetop, buttering a piece of bread. Landra looked up and smiled as she saw Jewel.

"You're awake."

Jewel nodded and looked around. "Where's David?"

"Work. We switched places late in the evening. He helped clean up a bit and I said I'd be here for the morning."

Wrapping her arms around her waist, Jewel moved towards the dining room of her one-bedroom apartment and took a seat.

"What day is it?"

Landra glanced towards Jewel hesitantly. She answered, "Saturday."

Jewel gasped and met her friend's eyes. "I've been here for a week?"

"Five days," Landra said grimly, she nodded and approached Jewel with the plate of toast. "I have an omelet browning on the stove when you're ready."

Taking the plate, Jewel sat it on the table and stared at the toasted bread before her. "Mr. Pierce," she said in a soft whisper.

"He knows. Whenever you're ready, you can just call accounting and they'll help you sort your days out."

Jewel nodded numbly. She lifted a slice of bread to her mouth and took a bite. The marmalade was sweet and thick. The crust scratched the roof of her mouth. She forced a swallow, realizing how hungry she really was. Jewel finished the piece of toast within a minute and immediately moved to the next.

Landra chuckled as she watched. "I take it you hadn't been eating much, huh?"

Jewel shook her head. "I need some water too."

"On it," Landra brought a cold glass of water to Jewel and sat it down promptly.

With another weak grin, Jewel took a deep sip. "This is so good, thank you," she continued to eat. Afterward, Landra brought the omelet to her. Jewel tore through the plump dish that was stuffed with onions, bell peppers, cheese and meat. She forgot how good of a cook her friend was.

Landra joined Jewel at the table with another plate of food, over easy eggs, toast, and a steaming cup of coffee. Together, they ate in silence.

"I'll never be able to repay you," Jewel said as she neared the end of her plate. Her friend smiled and shook her head lightly.

"You won't have to," she said softly. Landra took a deep breath and sipped on the coffee. "You may not feel very strong right now, but you are. You've been through a lot and you're so much stronger than you realize, Jewel." Landra's smile brightened. "I'm proud of you," she said confidently. "Underneath all the pain is a strong, beautiful woman. Guess that's why your momma nicknamed you Beautiful Jewel. You're a diamond in the rough."

25

The Real Healer

It was several more days before Jewel felt confident to return to work. In total, she missed six and a half days. David and Landra took turns keeping her company. They watched movies, played card games, and she and David talked late into the night.

Normal didn't return to Jewel until Wednesday, and even then, she still felt different. David said she would probably feel different for a while, now that she realized who she was and what happened in her past. They were eating lunch together at her favorite deli. Food and drinks had already arrived. Since the last Monday with Mr. Alura, Jewel had finally seen restful sleep. Occasionally, when she closed her eyes, she would see herself as that poor abandoned child locked in the room, but the image no longer brought confusion or mystery. She knew who she was.

"Have you thought more about calling Mr. Alura back?" David asked after a quick sip of cola.

Jewel shrugged. She had thought a lot about it, but never for very long. She didn't know how to respond to their last encounter. She ran away, ignored his phone calls and avoided the issue altogether.

"Honestly, I don't think I can face him again," Jewel admitted. She noticed that she found herself able to be more honest with David. Topics she would have once avoided, those which namely involved her feelings, she braved to discuss. She rarely offered too much information, but it was a step in the right direction, and it was one she knew David was extremely appreciative of.

David took in a deep, calculated breath. He watched Jewel carefully. "Why do you think you've been able to help so many women find personal healing, Jewel?" She lifted her eyes and met David's gaze. "You're an incredible therapist, Jewel. You might not have ever known it before, but somewhere, deep down inside, you've always been able to relate to their feelings, to their pain." He reached across the table and took her hands. "This is only going to make you stronger, baby. Mr. Alura can help you."

Jewel was captivated in the reality of David's words. They touched her somewhere, connecting with her consciousness in a way he hadn't been able to do before. She knew that he was right. She lowered her gaze and reached for her cup. Although she had been able to return to work, she asked that Lexy be reassigned. She was working only with older females now. She didn't think she could be that close to Samantha.

Her mind often traveled to that grungy mother. To think she endured the pain for a few hours while that poor child had known years of her grandfather's abuse. The thought only sickened her to the core. There was another thought that rattled

Jewel's mind. It was the fact that although the startling dreams proved to be the deepest secret of her unknown past, Jewel felt relief and a sense of thankfulness when she thought of Samantha. She realized that she was lucky. Even with the darkest day of her life that had plunged her into a living hell, she was still fortunate to have survived at all. She had known love and happiness from her family. Samantha had only known betrayal.

"I really think you should finish your sessions with Mr. Alura. Perhaps even pay for one or two of your own." Jewel met David's gaze again. She nodded quietly, knowing he was right. "So you'll do it?" He asked eagerly.

Jewel smiled slightly, something that was no longer a forced action. "Of course, babe. For you," she blew a small kiss. David caught it with his hand and touched his fingers to his lips. Jewel laughed.

Standing, David leaned over the table to plant a kiss on Jewel's lips. "This is only going to make you stronger and more effective," he pulled away and sat down. Jewel nodded. She didn't feel the truth of his words, but somewhere, she believed them to be honest and sincere.

After lunch, she made an appointment with Mr. Alura through his secretary. She was thankful for that middleman to book her appointment through. It was set for Friday, nearly two weeks since she had last seen him, and the thought still made her nervous.

She continued to update her case studies and work with support groups and personal counseling. David and Landra still made sure one of them gave her evening company, something she was eternally grateful for. Eventually, she knew she would have to get used to the silence in her own home again. With each passing day, that was a day she felt was coming sooner than later. Oddly enough, even though she knew her journey was far from over, she felt as though she had just crested a monumental hill in her life.

Before long, Jewel was back in Mr. Alura's office for her appointment. He greeted her as if having met for first the time. His eyes were kind and understanding.

Hesitantly, Jewel muttered, "I'm sorry about the other day."

He shook his head quickly. "Don't worry about it. I'm just glad that you returned. I'm very proud of you, Jewel."

She exhaled deeply. For some reason, those words meant so much more to her now than she ever recalled before. She remained quiet and looked over the quiet strength of his counseling room. She ran a hand through her hair and then crossed her arms over her chest.

"I just don't understand how I could have forgotten such a thing."

"Lacunar Amnesia," he responded quickly.

Jewel blinked. "That's right," she admitted. "I've heard about it—studied it in college." She chuckled at the revelation. "I just don't think I ever met anyone with it."

Mr. Alura nodded firmly. "When the body represses memories as a means of protection, they always find their way out. In your case, they came back through dreams, blackouts, visions, and memory loss." Jewel nodded again with a sigh. She didn't have anything else she could offer Mr. Alura. He cleared his throat with authority and continued. "You've more than likely have allowed this suppressed pain to manifest and dictate many of your decisions in your adult life."

"That's what a few of my friends have told me," she admitted softly. She chewed on her lip, thinking.

"It's been the source of your greatest successes. Your career. You do so well helping others who felt just as helpless as you did," Mr. Alura paused, "but it's also probably kept you back in other areas too."

"My relationships," Jewel breathed. Mr. Alura nodded knowingly. "I've never been able to keep a steady relationship with a man," she chuckled awkwardly, "even now, David is the best man I've been involved with and yet I've struggled for months with trying to offer him commitment."

"How would you say you've treated him?"

"Poorly," Jewel chortled. "Sometimes I've plain ignored his texts and calls and lied about it later. I think he knew too. But he never left me."

With another firm nod, Mr. Alura said, "This is how the negative aspects of childhood trauma affect adults in the present. It's caused you to sabotage your relationships."

"What?" Jewel blinked. Landra used that word with her not too long ago.

"You've purposefully acted in ways that would cause the end of your relationship. Maybe you didn't think you deserved them, or maybe you didn't think you could *trust* the people in your life," Mr. Alura shrugged. "Either way, when you sabotage relationships, it all ends the same way. You stay alone, and you feel alone."

Jewel nodded, hanging on to his every word. "That's me," she agreed. "How can I make it stop?" She looked down at herself, a bit disgusted. "I've helped nearly a hundred women over the course of my career with the counseling center. They've gotten married to good men; they've found good jobs. But me?" A strained laughed escaped her throat, "I can't seem to help myself."

Mr. Alura nodded. "Your brain has worked hard to block this memory for years, Jewel. Even though it happened 22 years ago, because of Lacunar Amnesia, it's like it just happened."

"It feels like it just happened," she choked out. She shook her head and looked down at her hands. "I have all the tools and yet, I feel like this thing is something I can't reach to touch. All my knowledge is useless. How? How can I do this?"

"You can't," Mr. Alura responded softly. "I can't heal you either," at his words, Jewel snapped her eyes towards his. "I can listen to your feelings, your emotions. I can help you process them. That'll help, but it won't heal," he shook his head. "I tell all my clients this, Jewel. True healing comes from the One who is able to touch those deep places that you mentioned, those dark, hidden places in your soul."

Jewel eyed him curiously. "You're talking about Jesus?"

Mr. Alura nodded. "Do you know him personally, Jewel?"

She nodded. "I do. My mother had a beautiful relationship with the Lord, she gave Him her life forever," Jewel sighed. "I know him as my Savior, but I feel so broken. Will this be with me until the day I die?" She met Mr. Alura's gaze. "I want to be able to laugh one day. I want to be able to smile and mean it."

"You want to be able to live."

"Yes," she hesitated, "can Jesus do that?"

Mr. Alura smiled. "He already has. He's used you to help you aid your clients as they navigated their own past pain towards complete and full healing. You know of how Jesus healed the physically afflicted, don't you?" Jewel nodded. Her hands were clasped firmly in her lap as she greedily devoured his words.

"He also helped those that were oppressed too, didn't he? It doesn't matter if it's physical or mental. Jesus is a healer, Jewel. Our healer."

Jewel considered his words. She looked down at her palms again. She believed in Jesus Christ. She recognized Him as her Lord and Savior, but in the later years of her life, the dreams and visions had gotten so bad that she was turned away. She didn't read her bible that often and had declining attendance in church. She had prayed and prayed for deliverance from the dreams for too many years it seemed. She never understood what He was waiting for. She had been suffering long before her memory had come back. Why hadn't he answered her prayers years ago? When she was begging and pleading for Him to intervene?

"The Lord wants to heal you, Jewel. As a therapist, I can help you make your way through the feelings and emotions. That's all anyone can do. But Your Lord, Jesus can heal your heart and make it new."

Jewel felt emotion swelling within her chest. "I want to be new," she whispered.

Mr. Alura nodded. "There is so much more that the Lord wishes to give you, Jewel—to show you. He's the one true counselor that will never fail. Are you ready to let him heal your soul?" Jewel nodded eagerly. Her eyes were wet again, but this time, she didn't feel so desperate, nor so alone.

Over the course of the next months, Jewel met with Mr. Alura often, at least once a week and in some cases, two. His guidance as a therapist helped Jewel to hone her own professional skills, but more importantly, he helped her sharpen her personal relationship with Jesus. He showed her how to study the scriptures and passages for herself and how to use them to strengthen her mind when she felt weak and struggled to discern the truth from a lie.

It wasn't an easy journey. There were many times that the visions came back and she felt deep pits of anger for what happened. During those times, David was there to help her through the feelings. She never realized how therapeutic it would be to talk through her intense feelings. It brought them closer together in a way she could have never imagined.

She had to acknowledge the truth about her past. That she was angry at her mother and father, and even Ms. Ella. She was furious at Ms. Ella and felt guilty for Samantha. When she realized the hidden anger for her parents, it only made her feel even guiltier. Mostly because she knew her father's heart. She knew how deeply her mother and father cared for her; but, it didn't keep a part of her from wondering why they never looked into what happened further.

The lie trying to embed itself in her mind was that if her parents really loved her, they would have sought help for her sooner. David and Mr. Alura helped her to see the flaw in that logic. They did help her as best they could. They removed her from the daycare. In fact, after her disappearance, her mother had even quit working for a year until she was old enough for school.

Back then, Jewel didn't understand why her mother quit her job. It put a financial strain on the family. There were several arguments about money and things were tight and strained, but the love within her family was stronger than ever.

David and Mr. Alura showed Jewel that her thoughts were false, that they were a lie. She knew people could think incorrectly. It happened all the time with abuse and especially with sexual abuse when her clients actually believed they deserved it. Because they *felt* and *thought* they deserved it, it made it incredibly difficult for them to achieve healing. Even though the lies convinced their minds that they deserved it, in their hearts, they still felt violated and wrongly taken advantage of. Those conflicting viewpoints follow victims everywhere because it hadn't been settled and healed.

It was only until Jewel could honestly believe with her head and her heart that she had done nothing to deserve it and that her family did everything they could to protect her with the information they had that the lies stopped surfacing. She found herself thinking more and more about Samantha, and how her life must have played out. She wondered how that innocent girl must have felt to realize that she was never protected by her grandmother because of fear.

Jewel always thought fear was such an interesting thing. It could keep even the best people with the purest of hearts from doing the right thing. It could cause the quirkiest of actions that often led to disorders such as OCD and terrible panic attacks. That's where Jewel was along the spectrum of dealing with her hidden pain, near panic attacks and social anxiety disorder.

As more time passed, she learned how thankful she was of Mr. Alura's help and friendship through the journey of forgiveness. They had stopped having counseling sessions weeks ago by the time she found herself outside of his practice building. They continued informal sessions on the phone when Jewel had a question or two that she didn't feel like bothering David with.

Jewel found that she approached David more and more about issues, and she consulted Mr. Alura less and less. That's when she realized that it was time. On this particular day, she had flowers she wanted to give as a thank you and a tribute to Mr. Alura's incredible work in her life.

At the front desk, Jewel cradled the flowers in her arms and smiled. It was a genuine smile, unforced and free, like her heart was now, completely free from the burden of her past.

Instead of the usual thin, fashionista who sat behind the glass, there was a short, plump older woman.

Jewel shrugged the thought away. "Is Mr. Alura in? I would like to give him these flowers as a thank you. I think our work together is finally done."

The short woman peered into Jewel's eyes. "I'm sorry, who?"

"Mr. Alura. He's been working with me in trauma counseling."

With a frown that dipped into the corners of her mouth, the woman looked Jewel over carefully. "Ma'am, there's been no one that has worked here by that name in the ten years that I've been here."

Jewel frowned this time and took a step back. She looked around the office and then back towards the receptionist again.

"Thomas Alura doesn't work here?"

"No, Ma'am. I'm afraid not."

"Oh," Jewel lowered her gaze, her cheeks burned with embarrassment. She squeezed the flowers into her chest and muttered a soft apology before she turned and left the building. Once outside, she looked back to the glass doors.

She turned and numbly walked towards her car. She didn't notice the figure waiting for her by the driver's side door until she heard a voice speaking to her.

"Hello, Jewel."

Jewel's head snapped towards the familiar, warm sound. "Mr. Alura?" Her eyes grew wide. Jewel pointed towards the building behind her and faced him with her mouth open.

He smiled and nodded knowingly. "I don't work there," he said calmly. "I never have. I work here," he touched his heart, "where it matters most."

Frowning, Jewel shook her head. "I don't understand."

"You let go of the guilt, Jewel," he said kindly. "You forgave yourself for those things that were sabotaging your life. They no long have power over you."

Jewel couldn't help but smile at the truth in his words. They settled over her with a comfort she hadn't known in a long time.

"You're free, Jewel."

"Yes," she nodded and sniffed. "I know. I brought you these flowers," she looked down at the bunch of flowers, daisies, and poppies in her hand. It wasn't much of a gift to give a man, but she felt it was appropriate. She lifted her head and held out her hands, but stopped. Mr. Alura was gone. She looked around, confused. There was no one around her, just a gentle breeze that blew through her hair.

26

Reunited

"Thank you for doing this," David whispered into his fiancé's ear. Jewel giggled back from the passenger's seat. She held onto David's arm and surveyed the two-story suburban home to the left of the street. She could already smell a warming grill and hear the cackle of loud laughs from the members of her family. Her brother would be somewhere in the back, probably manning the grill. From what she could remember about Keith, he always loved to cook. After graduating from culinary school, he worked along Chicago's top chefs before opening his own restaurant. Needless to say, he was always the cook at a family get together.

"I'm a little nervous," Jewel admitted, peering at the home. She couldn't see anyone, but she could hear the sounds of the fun they were having. The cookout started just over ten minutes ago and friends were still arriving. She had yet to tell her father that she would be joining them, as she wanted to keep it a surprise. Now, her stomach was tight with anticipation and worry.

"What if they're angry?" Jewel asked suddenly. She looked at David. "Do you think they'd be mad at me?"

He chuckled. "You're so cute when you worry," he kissed her forehead. "I'm sure they'd be happy you're here."

Jewel looked at the house again and nodded firmly. "You're right. Why do I let myself get worked up like this?"

"Because you want your daddy to like your soon-to-be-husband," he smirked and kissed Jewel again. It was her lips this time, and he pressed against her with all the love he had in his heart. He took her breath away. When he pulled back, she saw a deep desire and longing within his eyes.

"I love you, Jewel. Your family loves you too," his voice was a husky whisper. Jewel could only nod. "Are you ready to do this? Ready to let me meet your folks?"

Jewel giggled. She threw her arm around his neck and squeezed. He was the epitome of a man ready for marriage. He had been there for her when she needed him the most and then sometimes when she didn't. He looked forward to her future and wanted to be a part of it, relishing the unknown of what they could have together.

Releasing David, Jewel turned and opened the door. She leaped outside and shut it quickly. Probably a little too hard, but David didn't notice and only grinned at his bride-to-be's joy and beautiful heart.

He exited the vehicle and locked the doors. Holding hands, they crossed the street and approached the door to her father's house. David let Jewel knock on the door. As they waited, David gave Jewel's hand a friendly squeezed. She touched his arm and smiled at him, tilting her head to catch his eyes.

"I'm so glad I have you. You are my biggest blessing," she smiled brightly, beaming ear to ear.

They heard yelling from within the house. "If you were invited just come on in!"

Jewel giggled. They had already talked about waiting for someone to open the door. She was certain someone would soon enough, and she was right. Moments after the informal invitation to enter the home, someone swung the door open. They were holding a young child in their arms.

The man looked first at Jewel, David, and then back to Jewel with wide eyes.

"Baby Sis, is that you?"

Jewel giggled. "Keith?"

"Oh my gosh!" He yelled over his shoulder for his father, and then quickly leaned into Jewel for a hung. Tears stung her eyes as they pulled away. She took in the sight of the little girl nestled into his chest.

"Oh my, is this your daughter? Marissa?"

Keith blinked repeatedly. "You remembered," he said softly.

Jewel nodded. "Of course I'd remember my big brother's baby girl." They hugged again, but her attention was caught when an older man stepped into the doorway. Keith moved aside as he pulled his daughter into a tight embrace.

It had been years she had seen her father, but he was still the tall, strong, well-built man of his youth. His hair was sprinkled with salt and his face was worn, tired, but still true. His eyes beheld Jewel's.

"I didn't think you'd come," he breathed softly. He looked to David, unable to hide the grin that played across his face. "So you're him? The one that brought my baby back?"

David chuckled nervously, and then shook his head. "Jewel did this," David said quickly with a firm nod. "She's strong. That wasn't me, sir—."

"Oh, no you don't. Call me William or Dad. You're one of us now, son," her father pulled David into a tight embrace. Over his shoulder, he winked down at his daughter.

"My family is finally complete," William said in a burly voice on the edge of laughter and cries of joy. He pulled away from David and faced Jewel. "Thank you for coming home."

Jewel was crying with overflowing happiness. All these years she had convinced herself that the longer she stayed away, the longer her father, brother, and family would be upset. That was the lie, David had told her. Just as her mom and dad's love for her was great as a child, so too was their love great for her as an adult. That was the truth.

"Thank you for waiting for me," Jewel said through her tears. She leaned into her father and hugged, squeezing with all her might the missed hugs from years ago.

27

Pay it Forward

Jewel sat behind her desk and stared at a square sheet of paper. The daycare case had gone to trial and received a verdict. Mr. Alan Fuller was sentenced to a maximum security prison and 75 years behind the bars without parole. Jewel was sure that no one really expected him to live longer than a month within the facility. It was the next best thing to death row. Once other inmates discovered his crime, he was for sure a goner.

She didn't feel the type of elation she had expected that she might. Still, something else tugged at her heart. On the sheet of paper in front of her was a number she had never dialed.

Jewel lifted up the receiver and pressed it against her ear. She keyed in the numbers on the sheet of paper slowly and then held her breath. After two rings, someone answered the phone.

"Hello?"

Jewel wouldn't have been able to mistake that Midwestern draw for anything in the word. "Hello. Is this Samantha?"

Jewel heard breathing on the line. With hesitation, the woman answered. "Yes. This is she. Who is this?"

"It's me, Julianna Kennedy."

There was more silence, and then abruptly, Samantha muttered, "What do you want?"

Jewel's heart was beating fast, but not from fear. "I want to help you."

Samantha chuckled. "You can't help me. No one can."

"That's a lie," Jewel said softly. "I know because I used to think the same thing, Samantha."

There was another chortle. Jewel could tell that it was from anger. "What do you want?"

"I already told you. I want to help you, Samantha. When I was a scared little girl who thought she was all alone, you cared enough to make sure I was safe from your grandfather," Jewel breathed slowly and surely. "Since then I've had my own battles but I've prevailed and I've been victorious. Now it's my turn to help you find freedom, Samantha. I know you're hurting inside. No one saved you as you saved me."

There was a gasp of air through the line from Samantha. "My grandmother died two weeks ago," she said softly.

Jewel nodded. "I saw it in the obituaries." Ms. Fuller had committed suicide from pills. "I'm so sorry for your loss Samantha, but I don't want that to be you. Don't you want to be free?"

There was no mistaking it now. Samantha was crying. "Yes," she cried out. "Help me, please."

Jewel smiled. "Listen to me Samantha, this doesn't have to be your reality any longer. You don't have to live the rest of your life in pain and turmoil. You can live free and experience healing. I'll show you the way. Just like someone showed me."

Made in the USA
Charleston, SC
29 July 2015